MW01484702

Be
A
Pussy

By

Miriam Adams

Table of Contents

DEDICATION

This book is dedicated to the Kemetic (Egyptian Goddess) Bastet (Bast), daughter to Ra and wife to Ptah. She was often depicted as a woman with a cat/feline bust. Bast was known as the female panther/cat and protector of women, children, and domestic cats. She was notably given homage in the blockbuster hit Marvel's "Black Panter," where her prowess and power were displayed on the big screen. Bast was also connected to jars of perfumes and ointment and held a prominent position in the embalming process of mummification. She was a goddess of sunrise, music, dance, and pleasure, as well as family, fertility, and birth.

The people of ancient Kemet celebrated her with drums, music, good cheer, wine, and sensual dance. Like many of the great Kemetic Goddesses, she was fierce, resourceful, and acted within her own abilities, birthright, and independence. She was the first and ultimate Powerful **Pussy cat!**

Be a Pussy! *Guide*

The Independent Woman's ~~Vent~~ to Dating in the 21st Century

INTRODUCTION

What a woman lets slide into her vagina can either give her orgasmic bliss or ongoing phantom pains. As women, we seem to be the ones in the dark ages about the value of our little kittens. Men, on the other hand, are very much aware of the value of the pussy, which is why they are constantly trying to MANuever that mysterious portal. But let it be told by them, and those hairy little cookies are one of many in the jar, as the memes are stating these days. And we are buying these great marketing techniques from the very male-dominant society that puts them out there. Women are the ones still trying to write checks on their pussies when in fact, we are walking around with blockchain technology between our thighs. We are the ones not realizing what our vaginas really mean for us and the world around us. Let's face it; we have devalued our own vaginas because of what we allow to be done to them… and us! The manifestation of this is not more apparent anywhere than in the single and dating arena today. We are the ones being cowards. We can't blame men; they're just getting free pussy! Well, I don't know about you, but I have been a coward for far too long, and now, it's time to close shop, and none of that "going out of business sales" either!!

If you are anything like me; professional, smart, have a good career, independent, have your own car, a place to live, and have your other shit together, then you are either probably single or in a situtiationship with a non-committal man, or on the edge of being miserable, are miserable, lonely, or in denial about your loneliness! Hey, I'm still part of the "living my best life" crew tho. Kinda.

I wish I could tell you I have found the answer to snagging that champion man we were told existed in abundance. That champion of a man who will come to his senses and realize you are his long-lost princess whom he has found and searched the world over for. The same champion who will ride in on the dawn of morning and save you from a life of loneliness, heal your broken heart, and had you at hello. News flash, ladies, this fairytale is utter bullshit! And not just bullshit, but bullshit that only exists (quite possibly) in our imaginations and the movies. Do I sound pissed? Damn Straight! Hostile was the exact terminology the last guy I dated used about me. And for what? For having an opinion other than his and being as passionate about my opinions as he was about his. Somehow, as a woman, I wasn't supposed to express myself so blatantly, and mind you, I even left out cuss words while I expressed myself to him. Go figure, but I digress! Sounding like a true vent yet? Yep!

Yes, ladies, I wish I had some good answers for you on somehow miraculously being compatible with more men than you obviously are repelling, as there seems to be an array of single men available. Everyone is getting divorced these days, right? These men are out there, right? Well, yes, but can we say sloppy seconds? Baggage, to say the least, and/or have too many issues to count! And to be fair, we all have issues. I get this. But really, has dating become this difficult? Has finding a good man become but wishful thinking? I would like to think not, but my pessimism on this topic has cross-referenced with reality, and my experiences tell me that something's up. Some things have changed, a paradigm shift of sorts that we, as women, are not in tune with yet.

If you are like me, you have probably spent innumerable hours bawling your eyes out with a bottle of Moscato. The same bottle that the last guy you were seeing brought over. The same guy you were almost sure about was the one. You would have poured it out as an act of liberation from that man, but why waste cheap wine, really? And it wasn't even your favorite brand!

I'll admit I struggle with loneliness and being alone. I'm sorry, I'm not a personification of those ideal Facebook quotes about single women who have found peace in singledom, like being alone, and are gloriously happy being by their damn selves. I say to those quotes, Go suck it! I'm sure there are some women like this, but not many. And maybe by the end of this book, I would have changed my mind; who knows? I'm not sure at this point. The Living Your Best Life crew, going on vacation every other month, posing on IG, photoshopped photos to show the world just how glossy your life is, is a bit of a farce. Don't get me wrong; I love seeing people do wonderful and positive things and cheer for them. I like and love it with two thumbs up. I also love sharing my life with the world on my social media platforms for various business and personal reasons. However, there is a breach in reality at times that just may not translate the same from our IG pages to what's really REAL. I will go into more detail about this in the chapter on the real reality of social media.

Not only do I not have the answers, but I'm also beginning to wonder if there are any good answers as to why being a professional, independent, career-minded woman these days equates to being single and alone. I'm beginning to wonder if the answers will only infuriate me even more if I do happen to stumble upon them. I mean, aren't we the coveted women that we see in the movies and hear about in the media, who have the careers, who have their shit together for the most part, and that woman has a man! And even the third from the last guy you dated told you that he was looking for an independent woman who wasn't clingy, had her own interests, friends, and stuff, and wasn't the other "N" word. "Needy!" Isn't that what he said until you opened your mouth and could form a coherent sentence without expletives after every word? As soon as you opened your mouth and debated a subject just as intellectually as him, and as soon as you exerted your independence and knew how to get things done without much "dictation" from him, there began the back-peddling two-step dance. Now, I'm hostile!

There's something about a woman scorned. Back in the day, women would poison their men and take care of them while they were poisoning them. *Insert longing sigh here. But as forensics has gotten more elaborate, it's trending these days to just get creative in the arts, or however you like to express yourself when a man doesn't realize how wonderful you are. Just ask Mary J. Blige and Taylor Swift. They performed award-winning songs from their scornings. And Alanis Morissette, remember her; she sang the all-time female anthem on calling out male back peddling bullshit.

So, this is the thing, ladies. This book is not necessarily about finding the answers, although I will share some theories of mine as to why I believe so many professional, independent, and intelligent women like me and you are indeed single. This includes theories like "the myth of the Champion man" and "how we are operating from outdated definitions of male and female roles." But I will mostly explore my own thoughts, beliefs, half-truths, and temporary truths, forming truths based on my experiences and the things I am witnessing as a single woman in today's culture. And when I speak about being single, I mean those who are not married or in a committed relationship that's longer than a year. I know, ladies. I know three months is considered a long-term relationship these days.

In the chapter on online dating, we will go down the rabbit hole of serial/online dating issues that exacerbates our failure rates in record numbers and is quite possibly the spawn of the devil! We will also explore how we find ourselves on the quest for perfection and the Barbie Clone Syndrome while pondering if only we were even more perfect. If we just nip this and tuck that, implants, and disguise makeup, then maybe we could snag that perfect man for us. Amongst other explorations, we shall go on adventures down the yellow brick road, off the deep end, and possibly even make some wrong turns.

This book is my personal vent, guide, or rant, as some may call it, of me just trying to figure out, well… me. That and where I fit, and possibly other women like me, may fit in this whole dating scene and what it means to be single at this time in HIStory. There are no scientific measures, graphs, or doctor's stamps of approval in this book. There are no long hours of researching this statistic and that one, and you will even find made-up words that I like to use that are not in anyone's dictionary but my own. You may even think I have some violent tendencies lying dormant, and to that, I would say, doesn't most people? I also want to clarify that I'm not a physically violent person, but I can be verbally aggressive at times. Even that is mostly in a literary figurative manner. I'm a far better writer than an orator. And my last physical fight, I believe, was when I was five years old. I would even agree with you that some things I say in this book are probably utter bullshit. But then I would also add, isn't everyone peddling bullshit to some degree, and it really comes down to a matter of convincing people to believe your bullshit? I may even contradict myself at times throughout this book. Wow, it's unheard of for human beings to oscillate between concepts and thoughts. I'm not sure if one could ever not contradict themselves and have any form of growth in their lives; more bullshit? Possibly! Whose validation or proof do we need anyway, other than our own swollen, cried-out eyes from another failed attempt at finding our Champion and the rightful relationship we are supposed to be entangled in? I mean, aren't you and I entitled to a good, happy relationship as much as the next person? Yes, I'm a bit annoyed and angry. I am because we were told that if we were good little girls, got our homework done, weren't a hoe, worked, cleaned up our houses, and were family-oriented, then our Champion would come knocking down our damn doors to get to us. I don't know about your door, but mine hasn't had a quality man come knocking in a while. I just have pervs trying to peep through my windows and send me dick pics! Okay, that's a bit extreme!

I can already hear the critics now. This is man-bashing! No, I'm not man-bashing. I'm "no good ass man" bashing! I will explain this type of man and how we can distinguish him from a plain good man later in the book, which seems to take a skill set these days. For the most part, when I'm referring to men in negative terms, I am speaking about this "no good ass man," better known as the NGAM, or I may speak about another type of male species, the "douche bag," better known as DB. I will explain these types of men in detail and in conjunction with what I am coming to realize, what a plain good man may look like in modern American culture.

Sometimes, we just need to indulge ourselves with a good rant or vent, whether it makes sense or not. It's your senses and no one else's. It can give us that time to sort through some things. Find that creative spirit within us and focus on it; maybe something good could come from it. Although I may present a harsh truth, half-truth, or forming thought of my own damn opinion, I fervently advocate that others should present their opinions just as passionately. Hey, someone may even convince me to buy into their bullshit, and maybe we can write a collab book together next year. Who knows, really? I'm open, with some time on my hands, apparently.

So, ladies, don't flush that bottle of wine your ex brought over; pop it open, Independent Women of the 21st century, and journey with me into this female enlightened or unenlightened rant… I mean Guide! Let's be positive here. The Lord, the Universe, or whatever higher power you believe in knows we have been listening to male rants free of charge all these years. *Insert Viola Davis eye roll here.

Chapter One:
Male Champion: Mythical Creature At Large

Male Champion: AKA: Knight in shining armor. AKA: Tall, Dark, and Handsome. AKA: Prince Charming. A male-derived and fabricated term to indicate a near-perfect man.

Every girl dreams of having her prince come and rescue her. Whether he's swinging from vines in the jungle, swinging his money-padded penis like Eddie Murphy in Coming to America One and Two, or is an invisible apparition coming back to save his teary-eyed wife like Patrick Swayze in the movie Ghost. Remember these movies and the scores more like them? Um, we are not even going to discuss the amount of inflated ego it takes to come back from the dead to save the day just yet. Really!! Oh, ladies, we eat this shit up and are buying it at the regular price.

The Male Champion defined: He is tall, dark, and handsome. He is confident! A decision maker! A Leader! Independently wealthy! A bit elusive because only you can capture and tame him! Honest! Loyal! He also has a chiseled chin, a strong nose, and is moderately handsome. Very moderately handsome in some cases if he is working that money bag and confidence thing. Ladies, you know I'm telling the truth here! Let's stop lying to ourselves. We love a man with some money, and who likes to hold his package, which is part of this problem we find ourselves in. Oh, and I almost forgot; the Champion defined makes us have multiple orgasms over and over again. Laughing out loud here!

Just about every girl I know wants and longs for a man like the Champion defined. This concept of a man is imprinted in our young female minds very early on. From our parents to the media, the books we read, and even our educational systems. It is a very intentional program we have been put on that travels with us into adulthood.

What I have discovered is that although this is a male-created farce, it's also a farce women have come to accept as our own and is a recurring dream within our mind's eye. Only we can stop this dream for ourselves because it has turned into a nightmare for some, a crime documentary for others, and comedy for those of us who are on the pessimistic side of life. That's as close to an answer as I think I may get in this entire book.

We must stop believing that our male counterparts are going to save and protect us somehow. Save us from loneliness and lack of finances, and protect us from the outlaws of the community. Those days are gone, ladies. Things have changed significantly from the days of our fathers and grandfathers when the majority of men not only had a desire to have families and stay with them throughout their lives but had more incentives to do so. I would insert a statistic on the lack of men in the home these days, but why beat that dead horse? Google it for your damn self!

I do not know about you, but from my dating experiences, many of these men today cannot save themselves, let alone us. They live in their parent's basements, for crying out loud and have roommates at 35 and 40 years old. Really! Not to mention, they play video games into the wee hours of the morning. This Champion of a man that we think is out there seems to be more elusive than Big Foot: occasional sightings, leaves footprints at the supermarket, and a sample of hair at the gym, maybe. And if you are a single woman in your 30s, 40s, and up, then there is no getting around men who are now divorced or have left a long-term relationship. Baggage claim, please!

We must ask ourselves, why would men ever want us to stop believing this lie? It's to their benefit for us to think they are capable of more than they are. Only Champion men get that this is an unfair pedestal, but real Champion men are not available to us; they are married and taken. If a man is in his 30s, 40s, and older and is still wandering around single, then he is not a Champion man by default. Champion men do not give up on their team. They do not leave their team in mid-season or trade teams. Just ask Lebron James what he had to go through when he ditched his team; he is still paying for that cheat night. Again, just saying... And if that 30, 40, or 50-year-old man hasn't even found a team yet, well, shit, is there a need for further explanation here? Okay, a couple more: Michael Jordan and baseball; really? And when Garth Brooks became Chris Gaines and side-barred Country music? WTH! I rest my case. And yes, I'm from the mid-west Garth! Champions do not leave their teams, not without repercussions, at least. As independent women today, we must grasp this fact when dealing with single men of our time.

Some of these single guys may be cool; I will give them that. They may have a job, a car, maybe even a place of their own, but by the time they get to us, they are so freaking broken they are limping and have a twitch in their left retina from their previous relationships and failed marriages. And because we have a vagina, everything we do reminds them of that previous woman they were chained to. Sometimes these guys can be worse than the average douche. Because they are so jittery about committing to just about anything, let alone you. These men lie to themselves about what they really want and will lie to you for that same reason. At least with douchebags, for the most part, they are upfront. Oh, I hear the guys now; the same goes for you women! Well, maybe so, but this is my story, so go write your own damn book! I don't date women; I date men!

Now, where did this image of the male champion come from, and why are we still buying it when it is obvious he has moved somewhere in or around the Bermuda Triangle? Well, it's a man's world, ladies! They are the empowered majority, and any time you have a majority demographic, then things seem to always appear in their favor. They are always held in a bigger light than what they truly are. Four inches, really, but somehow, they have convinced us it's 6 inches. **Insert giggle here.

We are also still operating under old and outdated definitions of male and female roles. I will raise my hand; I'm a traditionalist by nature. Believe it or not, I like some defined roles between men and women. Really, Miss Hostile herself is a traditionalist? Yes, sorta. But then, I am a rather convoluted person, so take that as you may.

Either way, things have changed and are continuing to change, and it's wishful thinking of days of old when we are clearly in a new age and time. And thankfully so because days of old weren't all that glorious for us as women. In those old days, your brother, father, or husband could and would protect you from the town outlaws with riffle and all, standing at post all night on the prairie farm. But the same husband could also come inside, accuse you of riling up the neighbors, smack the shit out of you, and there was nothing you could do about it because we didn't have any rights as women back then. In today's world, there's no need for a man to protect us like that anymore; as women, we have learned to protect ourselves and know how to shoot a damn gun, too! But it still is a great thought and gesture for our men to want to physically protect us; it still makes us fuzzy inside as women when they get all testosteroney like that. And as indicated, that same testosterone could turn aggressive towards us, as well as abusive. We did not have rights from any man back then, including family and husbands. We have laws that govern the land now, and that type of physical protection is not in great demand. Okay, I'm not saying that if I'm confronted by a male in an aggressive manner, I don't want my man to step up. He better, and hopefully, take the other dude out! But what I'm saying is that I'm not going to stand off to the side clutching my arms and watch my man possibly get the dog shit beaten out of him. No, as a woman of the 21st century, I'm going to pepper spray the MFer so that my guy can get another good hit on him, and maybe I can get a swift kick in there, too, that I learned in my kickboxing class. At least that's how it goes down in my mind; remember, I haven't been in a physical fight since I was like five years old.

My point, as independent women is that we want to be a help-mate to men these days. To be an equal, an ally, a fighting partner. But it seems the more we exert this help, the more we get pushed away. Why? Well, men, too, are operating under old, outdated definitions and concepts of what makes a woman a woman. Some men only see women as extensions of themselves, some think they are honestly smarter than all women, and some even go as far as believing they have a divine right to exercise authority over women. Again, being somewhat of a traditionalist, I love being feminine and, at times, stroking the male ego. I can even indulge and be the "S" word (Submissive) at times. Letting the man be the man, whatever that means. But I also know that I am my own person, independent from others, male and female. I don't have to depend on a man to make my decisions for me, nor is his decision-making somehow better than mine, as American culture has historically placed men in that lead role. What I have discovered is that quite a few men like that role, even if they are terrible decision-makers.

Many guys want the Glory of a Champion man and a woman to see them as a champion but are unwilling to do the work of a true Champion man. Unfortunately, men are set up in a way in our culture that they can demand more than they give, and some men take full advantage of that tax credit.

A true Champion man knows and understands that the concept of women is changing in everyday society. These men have accepted their women as the strong, independent women they are, which is why they are not single. These men have come to want and desire the value of a strong woman and how she can add to their lives. A weak man will always perceive an independent woman who has her shit together and is intelligent as someone thinking too highly of herself and high-minded. A weak man will always want to knock that woman down a peg or two. A true champion finds his strong, confident woman sexy in her assertiveness, not emasculating, and that's not to say that some women don't take a bit of power overboard and can be emasculating to men. Yes, this does happen. Just like we have immature men, we have immature women out there as well. Women who will abuse their power. A woman who has a good, sound, stable, and solid man will not feel the need to exert herself to that man in this manner. Again, it can come down to perceptions and definitions of how we filter others by our own experiences in life. What I mean by this is we all have our own set of ideals and beliefs, and we apply that not only to the world around us but to our significant others as well. Those perceptions are not always right. A no-good-ass or weak man will oscillate back and forth on what he wants from a woman. One minute, he will say he wants a strong, independent woman; in the next relationship, he will want a passive woman. Yes, many men are still operating under these old, stale definitions of who and what a woman is. As women continue to level up with men in this country, men must bring up their thinking to accept women as their equals even though we are probably a higher being than them. Yes, I snuck that in there. We all have things that we do better than the next person, for that matter. Men should not hold the role of knowing or doing "Best" just because they are men. The same goes for our romantic relationships. Culturally, men must come to this conclusion where women are concerned. Too many of them are inconsiderate in even addressing how they view women. Many will say that a woman is equal to a man, but their actions belie their words.

Only a weak man wants a weak woman. The true Champion man understands that a woman of today must be vocal, assertive, and confident to maneuver in this society if she is to succeed, and a true Champion man is not intimidated by this but welcomes this. He accepts the 21st-century woman is not an extension of himself, his property to do as he will, but who is her own person with her own mind. That champion man accepts women making decisions separate from him, and she can collaborate with him if she

18

likes. A man who is either an all-and-out douche or struggling with his own masculinity will always perceive a strong independent woman as a threat to his masculinity, as if she is trying to "muscle" him or assert herself above him. Only a weak man must keep a woman beneath or below him. A true champion accepts his woman as his equal and doesn't get bent out of shape when she is assertive and is her own person; he is proud of her and how she can get shit done!

As indicated above, and not to get too technical and researchy here, but things have changed from the days of our grandparents regarding women entering the workforce more in the mid-last century. We have heard the rumors and statistics on how women entering the workforce changed the family dynamic of male authority and child-rearing roles… yada, yada, yada. Let the men say: "See, the woman just had to go ruin things. Again!" They will never let us live down the whole Eve and Apple thing, either. Ever! Whether Christian or not, we get the blame for everything, even the beginning of it all. Well, Champion wannabes, after so many years of being oppressed by male authority, not being able to own property, being bought and sold, literally in my case (see my picture on the back cover, and this will make more sense to you) like cattle to the highest bidder. Who wouldn't get tired of this type of substandard life? It's the laws of nature or something like that, that oppressed people, whether women or men, will eventually revolt against their oppressors. Again, Google it!

Most guys, douchebag or not, know they can no longer live up to these unrealistic expectations, but so many still struggle to accept help from an independent woman and sometimes compete with us instead of allying up. But again, when things play in your favor to a certain degree, and there are some benefits to a lie, sometimes you just go along with it. Some guys are just caught up in the system and unsure what direction they should take with women and relationships. I tend to think of the word "Integrity," but that's just me. We get it, guys. It's kinda like when the store clerk gives you too much money back; for a split second, you almost let them know and give it back, but then you think about what you can do with it, so you keep the money and go your merry way. It's not your fault; they shouldn't have been such a dumbass is what you think. We understand; some guys just don't know why women continually put them on these unrealistic pedestals, and Susie Q. Dumbass is left crying, "I can't believe he cheated on me three times!" Well, that's just the three that you know about, honey!

But you know what, ladies, lack of integrity dude is right to a certain degree. We are being a bit dumbassy here. Like the store clerk, we are just not paying attention and counting the money right. Not only that, but we have also not realized that the currency has changed altogether (checks vs blockchain). It's not that the Champion doesn't exist, but we have to come to the conclusion that when you get to your 30s, 40s, and up and you are single, then that Champion man that we dreamed of has basically left the building. The Champ is down, and it's time for some emergency planning. Instead, what we continue to do is that we either chase behind him or wish he would come back for us on that white horse and carriage we read about. And then we start mentally raping ourselves. We must not be good enough. Something must be wrong with us. If only we could make ourselves better, more appealing somehow! We even start throwing more shade at other women because of our insecurities about ourselves as women. We start considering drastic measures to fill a void so that we can be more competitive for a man. And there we find ourselves in a never-ending cycle. A quest of sorts, the one that few achieve, some get close to, and others may even die for. The Quest for 36-24-36.

Chapter Two:
Barbie Clone Syndrome: 36-24-36…The Quest

Vaginal cosmetic surgery, WTF!!! Bootie Implants! This is how off the deep end we are going, ladies!! Obviously, this chapter is about how far we are willing to go to be perfect and what we are doing to snag and "keep" a man. I know we go on and on about how these invasive and dangerous surgeries are for US! Really now?! We will save the trending "Mommy Makeover" for the very end of this chapter. My question continues to be: Who are you trying to be perfect for? Is it really for you? It sure as hell shouldn't be for Ken because we have established from the last chapter that the Champion no longer lives in our neighborhood! You mean to be perfect for lack of integrity dude, with the missing left nut, the retina twitch, the crooked toe, and who will not commit to you and stop cheating? That guy!? Because common sense tells me that a man who loves us for who we are would never put pressure on us to get freaking vaginal surgery because our vajayjays just aren't pretty anymore. Just thinking about someone feeling that way, whether a man or woman, makes me want to vomit! Who gives a flying shit if your muffin isn't pretty? And even more so, who are the F'ing vagina police and inspectors? These MFers need to be arrested and stoned in the public square.

I think many of us who still have an ounce of sanity can agree that if we have gotten to the point where we need to have politically correct vaginas, things have gotten terribly off somewhere. But nonetheless, we are still on this quest to obtain our own come-to-life Barbie dream. We will go to great lengths to be the perfect woman for a man who's not even sticking around or trying to be this perfect woman that we think will make us happier with ourselves.

We all have heard about the true measurements of Barbie, were she a real woman, 39-21-33, which I think we can agree is a freaking Alien. She'd have a large head that she couldn't even hold up on her stick-thin neck; she wouldn't be able to bear children because of her deformed pelvic bones that give her the unrealistically small waist; she also would not be able to walk because her anorexic ankles could not support her. And most importantly, she wouldn't be able to talk because of the weight of her enormous boobs on her larynx, which would mean she could not nag a man… She's a keeper! I don't even need to mention here that there's a market for blow-up dolls or life-size, anatomically correct dolls for a certain male demographic: BKA: Sex Dolls! That's none of my business, *Insert, SICK BASTARDS here, sipping my tea.

There's also the measurements of the ideal woman floating around, the 36'-24'-36' woman. Although this is obtainable for some women, it is still unrealistic for quite a few others. First off, I want to say I am a fabulous woman. I would hope that all women thought of themselves along these lines. My definition of a fabulous woman is a woman who is moderate to very confident, who celebrates other women, who is independent, and takes care of herself: mind, body, and soul. She also does everything she knows to balance a life with her man, family, and children. There is nothing wrong with wanting to look good and what that means to you. There's nothing wrong with working out and taking care of your body physically. I am a big advocate for this. But we must know where the line is, what is beautiful, what makes us feel good, and even more importantly, why it does. This is where personal responsibility and preferences come in.

In all fairness, it's not just the guys playing a role in this madness. It is primarily us as ladies putting this kind of pressure on ourselves or reacting to these social cues about beauty, perfection, and youth. We are literally buying into this hype; some of us are going broke trying to be part of this inner circle, and some are even dying to feel pretty... and I don't mean that figuratively.

We have young girls and women starving themselves to stay thin; bulimia and anorexia are still not coming to the table on this issue... a twisted pun but true. And now, we are hearing about the space between the girl's thighs, which must be a certain distance in diameter from one thigh to the next for her to be in the cool kids' club. Look, I'm glad girls are putting math into perspective, but I'm pretty sure our math teachers didn't have this in mind. Or now, as I write these words, it is trending to "waist train." Really ladies? We fought for women's suffrage to rid ourselves of those damn constricting corsets, and now we are putting ourselves back into them! I have even gone back and forth with myself about that damn waist jail, and the buttocks implants have taken on a life of their bouncing own. Women deforming their bodies into these unrealistic and certainly not obtainable and maintainable forms. As women, it is natural for us to have a thicker, softer waistline and butt. It's okay to be slim also, but it is most natural for us to have a larger waist solely due to childbearing. Why do we want to look like pubescent boys by the waist? I'm going to leave that one alone. I will get more controversial in a later chapter, so brace yourself.

Just go through YouTube and TicTok reels and watch some of the videos our young and older people are putting out there. I must give credit to some of these folks. I especially like seeing young people being innovative, creative, and out of the box. There is nothing wrong with this. The creativity some of these young girls are doing with their hair, makeup, and clothes is fantastic for the most part. But just as there is an abundance of great videos on YouTube and Reels that I have gotten some very good tips from watching, there are also some very twisted and warped videos on there in abundance as well. I will cover more details on online media and a loss of reality in a later chapter, but go see some of these videos on makeup applications. Maybe I'm the one out of touch with the latest trends, but my everyday application of makeup isn't nearly as meticulous as some of these ladies and girls. i want to highlight here that I'm a girlie girl myself when it comes to makeup, hair, clothes, and all that; I love that stuff. But even for me, some of this seems a bit excessive. Everyday makeup wear has become photoshoot-ready and a disguise ploy. Again, I could be the one out of touch here. I didn't know the paparazzi were now just hanging outside of the average woman's home, ready to catch her in action. Maybe that's where I'm going wrong with this whole snagging-a-man thing!!

And yes, these social cues are being instigated by a male-dominated society, a commercialized society, and a beauty and youth-crazed society. We must understand that money and propaganda are running buddies; they are roadies! But again, as women, we need to wake up to this stuff, start using some common sense in these matters, and weed out for ourselves what is healthy and what is not. Cosmetic booty implants are not healthy, physically or mentally!

I'm not perfect, and we all have some hang-ups and insecurities. But what's funny is how women seem to be more accepting of a man's physical shortcomings, but when it comes to the physical attributes of women, men don't seem to be so forgiving or fair. At least, that's our perception. A woman must be a hottie, a babe, fine, thin, fit, with perfect nails and hair, yet that guy isn't the biggest catch by any means. He can have a gut, hair on his back, crooked left baby toe, crusty feet, a missing left nut, and yet we are supposed to accept these things about men without question. Nowadays, your average man believes and will be quite vocal about how he deserves these hot babes and will discard an average to a pretty woman with a few shortcomings on his hunt for the bigger, better catch. Or if that man has some money, then it becomes whom he can buy. Guys are fine with buying women. And we know this. It's part of this crazy cycle we are all finding ourselves in, and although some men, out of guilt, will say they are accepting of their women's shortcomings or what is perceived as a shortcoming by societal standards. Like if his woman gains some weight, most will never admit they left their wives or long-term relationships because of those few pounds. Even they know how shallow they must be to disrupt their entire family and leave their children because of a few fat cells. But I think we will be amazed if we were to delve into a man's psyche as to how many today are actually doing this. They are buying into this media hype that they, for some reason, deserve these "Real Housewives" types but, in reality, are just negatively focusing on their woman's "shortcomings." While that woman, on the other hand, has accepted everything about that man, and if he is good to her, that woman would be more than happy to stay with him and fight for her relationship. And here is Ken's third cousin removed, expecting you to be perfect. GTFOH!

Listen up, ladies and fellas, on this quest for perfection, one very blatant common-sense revelation has helped me to connect the dots on how beauty and perfection make very little impact on keeping a man happy. This enlightenment comes from the media and entertainment world itself: Halle Berry and Sandra Bullock. I think most would agree that these women are two of the most beautiful women on the planet, on The Planet! These ladies have their careers, are rich, have their own shit, and are Barbie. But they have men cheating on them, not staying with them, publically failed relationships, embarrassed by their once heralded Champions. Sounds familiar? Yikes, if Halle Berry and Sandra Bullock can't make a man act right, hell, we are doomed! What man in his right mind would leave Halle Berry? And who is better looking than Sandra Bullock and Halle Berry? This leads me to another blatant common-sense revelation, a reality that resides right here in our everyday world with the average everyday woman.

Many of us have encountered the average woman. Many of us are the average, everyday woman. This woman may have a few extra pounds on her, some stretch marks, average education, a decent job, and kids who are moderately well-behaved. And this woman has had her man with her from the beginning. He has never left her side. There is just no rhyme or reason to this madness! What is her secret? How did she get her man to stay when Halle and Sandra could not?

My conclusion: Absolutely nothing! There is nothing a woman can do to make a man stay with her. There is nothing a woman can do to make a man love her and never leave her. I know this is contrary to all the self-help books and lists of shit you should and could do to "keep" a man. And let the choir sing: Bullshit! It doesn't matter if you have the perfect coochie, the perfect set of boobies, are rich, have stretch marks, thin, fat, or fit. If a man does not love you for who you are, he will never love you. If he does not accept you for who you are and what you have to offer, he will never, and he will not commit to you. It is not our responsibility to take on a man's commitment and loyalty level! That belongs to that man all by himself. Simple, and yet very profound. End of story. I could end this book right here, huh? Nope, sorry, ladies, we are still not grasping something. All of this is common-sense stuff, yet we continue to chase the Barbie dream and skip down that yellow brick road, searching for our wizard who will make us perfect and whole. I don't know about you, but I just cannot shed another tear for another douchebag and will certainly not continue to put undue pressure on myself.

The media is a big culprit in peddling these ideals to us as to what is perfect and how women should behave and look. They are even feeding us on how men should treat women because of their looks. A male-controlled media outlet, mind you. We see on all these reality shows where women are tearing each other apart because of a "no good ass man" who is playing them both. And we are the ones watching this stuff. I was guilty of it, too, until I stopped my cable service. This competition for male attention, degrading and putting down other women to obtain it, is ridiculous. Most average everyday women wouldn't dare do these things and do not want to. So, why are there so many television shows showcasing this narrative? Well, I have also come to the conclusion there is a lot of power in keeping ignorance alive and pulsating. Lack of information and education is one of the biggest instruments of control around and has always been. The ultimate win is getting the demographic that's getting exploited to accept the exploitation and then join in with exploiting themselves. Genius!!

Now, on to this "Mommy Makeover" bullshit! Mothers… Wombman, listen up here! Why would you ever need a "mother makeover?" Even the words are counter to the divineness in you. As a mother, you never need a makeover or a do-over. We cannot buy into these marketing tools that are literally killing us. As I edit this chapter, another funeral just passed for a young celebrity mother who lost her life on the table of these dangerous surgeries. Please, women, mothers, just STOP! TURN OFF THE MEDIA! TUNE OUT THE COMPARISONS! LOVE YOU FOR YOU! It's not worth it. These invasive surgeries are mutilating women and taking them away from their families and children.

So, independent women of the 21st century, why are we striving to be perfect for someone who is by no means perfect for us and has very little pressure in society to be perfect for us? And who said we want perfection anyway? Does perfection equal happiness? Again, we have people in society whom we tote as nearly perfect by human standards, Halle and Sandra, yet they have failed relationships and problems like the rest of us. What else aren't we getting about being single, dating, and finding love in the new millennium? How is it that our self-esteem is getting lower and lower, possibly sending us running for surgical tables at the expense of our lives? Could some of our answers be enfolded in the idea of the man we are attracted to? Is the man you have in your life pouring into you or only withdrawing from you? Sometimes, what we are attracted to and what we are attracting can be two very different things. This dichotomy certainly has an impact on us. Or maybe the answer lies within us, how we view ourselves, our upbringing, and things we saw and were taught as children. We know it's quite possibly both along with a plethora of other things that have added to our life experiences. I'm not sure, but more exploration is necessary as we are not getting it yet. Ask any woman on the streets, and she will list out a few things she does not like about herself. Watch any commercial on media, and it's telling you something is wrong with you, and here's how you can fix it. We can only take in so much of that adverse information before our subconscious and conscious mind starts to believe it. I'm all about improving ourselves, our bodies, our minds, our spirits. With my coaching business, I harangue my clients into understanding the power of loving themselves at every phase of their lives. The love of who our natural self is, is the pinnacle of health. When we are healthy in mind, body, and spirit, we tend to make the best decisions for ourselves. We learn to set healthy boundaries with others and know how and when to say no without beating ourselves up. And we are not so easily manipulated by the media tactics to tear us apart. In a capitalistic culture, the more unhealthy you are, the more ignorant you are, the more unhappy you are, and the more you become susceptible to making money for other people. Again, there's nothing wrong with wanting to improve yourself for your own sake. Let's practice more self-love and positive affirmations daily. Throw Barbie and her measurements in the trash!

Chapter Three:
Independent Woman And The Manly Man: Oxymoron And The Clean Idiot!

The thought that it is an oxymoron to find an independent woman with a "manly man" is the exploration of this chapter. Many independent women like myself want this type of man. A man who can "handle" us, a man who takes charge, and a man we cannot walk over due to our strong personalities, which is not our intention in most cases. I think for us to really gather any understanding about the type of man we want and or attract, we must first define some things about ourselves. I must first define who I think I am and then define who this manly man is to me.

Let me start by sharing a picture of myself as I see myself and how I think others may see me. I would like to think that others see me as an independent woman. Well, when most people describe me, they use the word independent, and I have been accused by some of the male species as the "I" word as well. I am a decision maker, which I have discovered is the politically correct term for controlling bitch. I am disciplined. I am organized for the most part. I am resourceful. I am competitive. I am passionate. I am not afraid of conflict, and it doesn't bother me that other people may disagree with me. How they disagree can ruffle me a bit, but that's another book entirely. So, I'm pretty sure by American cultural definition, I am a man.

But before I get into how having these attributes can and has affected my romantic relationships with the human species with the penis, I want to first explain how all this has come to be within me and has helped to define me as the woman I am today. I encourage every woman to do the following:

Miriam, in a few words: I was the procreation result of my mother's affair with a married man. I have no memory of my biological father to this day. My formative years were spent in the high-rise projects of Chicago. I probably should have been murdered, raped, or severely injured by age five, but by the Grace of God and the Universe I was not. I was raised by a single mother who worked odd hours. She was very independent and resourceful herself and did the best she could as a single mother of four. She wasn't a perfect mother by any means, and I believe her to have been a functioning alcoholic for many years. My siblings and I were the latchkey kids of the 70s and 80s. I witnessed all kinds of urban madness that you could possibly imagine. We finally escaped to a small Midwest town before I was twelve and saw a unique way of living that I would eventually come to see as a hostage situation called white suburbia. I survived several years of childhood molestation by one of my mom's boyfriends that involved touching and fondling. I was the first of my mother's children to graduate high school and then college. My mother married a wonderful man in my pre-teen years who showed me what a father looked like. I Lost my mother to cancer during my freshman year in college. Had my son at the end of my freshmen year, dropped out of college after that, but went back the following year. I watched drug addiction claim all three of my siblings over a period of decades. My sister was able to find recovery and is still in recovery to this day. Both of my brothers remained under drug addiction, and for years, we were unsure if one of them was even still alive as we had not heard from him in years. Thankfully, in the last few years, there was a reconnection. However, at the beginning of 2023 and in the editing of this book, a stroke and possible drug-induced heart attack claimed my oldest brother's life. And my other brother, whom I love dearly, is an open homosexual and lives a life of homelessness. He, too, remains estranged from our family for going on five years now. My stepfather stayed with us even after my mother's death and gave my son someone to call "PawPaw." My son held his hand when he transitioned from this world to the next. I was with a man and married for ten years, divorced for 14 years now. My son graduated college in 2016, the first man in our family to graduate college in decades. I have been in my career field of Human and Social Service for 25 plus years. Presently, as I do my hundredth umpteen edit, I am self-employed as a Notary Public in the Real Estate Industry. I have no drug addictions and no STDs that have come out yet, lol. I do like a glass of Brut Champagne at social outings or when hanging with friends. I am not a functioning alcoholic, and to prove to myself that I am not, I go on 60 to 90-day alcohol fasts at a time, just to air on the safe side! I have struggled with panic attacks since my 20s and have been able to manage them without medications. Since moving to sunny California and a massive change in my diet, I have not had a panic attack in over five years. I am terrible with money and finances, although I have always been able to have it and do almost anything I want in life. I do have stretch marks that I hate. And if I could ever save enough money, I would likely get lipo suction, but I would never do anything to my face. At least, I don't think I would. Never say never. I have considered myself part of the Christian community most of my life, but I have since discovered that I do not like a great many of them. I follow an ancient African spiritual system called Ma'at, where the divine feminine is also exalted. I believe in collective Black Consciousness for African Liberation and black African diaspora community growth. At 51 years old, I have come to understand that spiritual and religious organizations are first cousins and human beings love power over other human beings. I am currently in the best health of my life and in better health than most my age. I have run a half marathon every year over the last ten years, except for the pandemic years. I survived the "scamdemic." I believe in natural immunity vehemently. I do not go to Western doctors nor engage in Western medicine if I can avoid it. From my mid-twenties to mid-thirties, I was a vegetarian. I had also been a pescatarian for close to 5 years and then became plant-based for a few years. I wasn't feeling the best and kept gaining weight while doing the plant-based diet, and didn't know why. I am now a Keto Carnivore who has lost over 30 pounds, feeling great, and again in the best shape of my life at 51. I am a Keto and Intermittent Fasting Coach and have coached numerous people on weight management and taking control of their health. In 2016, I made the leap and moved to Los Angeles, California, where my life had changed significantly, so much so that in my editing this very section, I have had to make more updates about myself as I have grown since the inception of this book in 2014 when I started penning it.

I think this is a standard American life… any romantic takers? And I will edit here that I did have a special man in my life for a number of years, and whom I loved. We had broken up and gotten back together more times than what is probably legal. We are on a break as I edit this section (AGAIN), but, in all my independence, I AM NOT A MARRIED WOMAN, and my belief is that I am single until I am married. I am not married by choice because apparently, there are just some things still missing for that to happen for me and for me to decide into marriage with a solid partner. I will leave that right there.

Again, I encourage everyone to write their life in a nutshell like this. There is no right or wrong way; just write what you want and feel at that moment. When we do this, we can begin to see how our basic personality is shaped and formed from this little writing exercise. Where some of our principles and morals may come from. The forming of our beliefs and ideals. But be mindful, if we are still alive on this earth, we still have plenty of living to do. This means there will be more to add, possibly more change, and forming to be experienced. You can also do this exercise as many times as you like with different information revealed about yourself over the years.

From all that I have shared above, it really shouldn't be a wonder as to why I would be searching for a Champion man! A savior of sorts in the form of a man? Is it really a surprise how I could warp the ideal of what constitutes a man in my mind? Not to mention my propensity towards creating fictional stories as a published author of women's fiction… yeah, I left that piece out above. Only one book published, though, but oh, was it a glorious escape into Lala land that included horse and carriage, Champion man, and a happy ending that even resulted in a planned pregnancy. Again, ignorance is a blissful bastard!

So, ladies, we must admit if we find ourselves in one failed relationship after another, we are the common denominator in those relationships. We must be willing to explore our definition of the man we want in our lives and how that definition was formed. We must be willing to admit the definition could possibly be off and not right for us. And often, we form our definitions in our mind about this man from how we view ourselves or how others view us.

Who is this man I see myself within my mind's eye? For me, I have always envisioned myself with the quintessential "Manly Man" who looms in the corners of my subconscious peripheral vision." He is very much like the general champion man of most women's dreams but tailored to my likes and dislikes. Not every woman wants the same type of man physically or emotionally. This, you must find out for yourself. You may find that some of your requirements or requests are like mine or very different.

I want to start with the physical, as the physique of a person is always the hook for us or bait and switch, something like that. Anyway, there's the physical attraction that grabs our attention.

"Manly man" defined: he is taller than me, preferably 6' feet tall or taller, broad-shouldered with a medium to stocky build, a few muscles are always nice but not required, and he is moderately handsome. Morris Chestnut is great to look at, but I don't require that type of physical eye candy. I'm not that far gone down the unrealistic trail, although some women are. I honestly do not ask nor require too much in the looks department. And with the physical, I generally get close to this type of man in my relationships with minimal problems. Now, where things get a bit turbulent in this manly man that I desire resides in the personality and character department and how he interacts with my independent self.

The personality of my manly man defined: He typically oozes confidence which I like. He borders on being a bit arrogant and maybe even cocky. He can be older than me; I have gone as old as ten years. As I have gotten older, that age gap has lessened significantly. His education is equal to mine or higher. *Pretty standard so far.* He can be demanding, and I am fine with this if he is nice about it. He can even tell me what to do if he asks gently. *You are probably feeling a wee bit of turbulence rumbling now*…hold on. This manly man likes to wear the pants, if he also doesn't mind me wearing mine. *Rumbling, Rumbling.* He likes being the leader and making the decisions, but only if he can let me lead and make decisions as well. *The plane is going into a nosedive position at this point.* Mr. Manly Man can also be a bit possessive of me, even jealous at times, but he dares not accuse me of a damn thing! *And so typically, at this junction, the plane and relationship are crashing in flames.*

I must ask myself, why? I think it's obvious that my desire for this type of man is a bit unrealistic, as many single women's definitions are. A manly man, by default, doesn't get along well with an independent woman. And although the burden of understanding this masculine male prototype is on us, society also plays a role in defining and forming this man. There is absolutely nothing wrong with a masculine male prototype and wanting one for yourself. Or even for a man to aspire to this. Often, Champion men have manly man qualities or exude masculinity. But often, with this manly man prototype, there is too much preoccupation on his part with masculinity, which can suggest that his masculinity is likely fragile. And this man could be threatened by the slightest exertion a woman may display of her power. Remember, Champion men are not threatened by a powerful, confident woman. The manly man generally likes being in the pilot seat without co-pilots. He's running this operation, and a man with this type of nature is rarely dualistic as to what I want and need. If this type of man exists as a single, it is in very small numbers. And when he exists at all, he's probably already in a committed long-term relationship as a Champion man to his woman.

Nine times out of ten, when I end up with a man like this, he always perceives me as controlling, aggressive, and just too damn independent, and I pretty much perceive him in the same light. But oh, do I love a man like this. It's madness. Why can't I have my manly man who is a leader, a decision maker, likes to run the show, can tell me what to do but be diplomatic about it, and can be possessive but not overbearing? Well, because I'm a leader and decision-maker and like to run shit!

You see, an independent woman like me and a manly man is an oxymoron. And the clean idiot is? Well, me! Because why would I ever think this type of man was out there in droves and lining up to woo me? I must conclude again that, on average, this man I want exists in small numbers, and the odds are slim that we would ever even meet on a romantic level, at least. I wouldn't go as far as to say I couldn't be in a relationship with this man I want, but he would have to be exceptional. That champion man, that 2% of men that may fit me well. The problem is finding him or waiting for him to find me. Do I wait, or do I figure out another type of man to be with, to settle on? Or do I become what my manly man needs by changing myself to fit him so that he stays with me and does not find me too overbearing? Well, I think we have pretty much gathered there's nothing we can change about ourselves to make someone love us or stay with us; remember Sandra Bullock and Halle Berry, yeah! So, I think our answer is clear. We either settle or we wait. That's a depressing ass thought and conclusion, I must say! And since this is getting too depressing and deep, and I am currently not married and have not found this verifiable man yet, let's move on to the next chapter. What I want in a man, what I am attracting, is something I must continue to explore. And if you are currently single or unmarried, you may want to continue to explore these definitions you have: who you are attracting to you and why. I do believe the more we explore and come to terms with what we want, the better we may become at attracting the man who could be good for us. Maybe we will explore waiting and settling later in another chapter; at this moment, I haven't decided yet. I'm even wondering if we could ascertain if a particular man is good and right for us without first being in a relationship with that type of man.

I will interject here some clarification on being unmarried and being in a committed long-term relationship. I do not believe marriage is the quintessential indicator of a happy relationship, but I do believe it is a verifiable step in long-term commitment. I also know people can be in a long-term relationship that is more productive than a legal marriage. If that relationship is meeting your higher needs and wants in life, then it is the relationship for you. If you are in a married or long-term relationship and it is not serving your higher needs and wants in life, then it is likely not the best relationship for you.

In the meantime, of waiting and/or figuring out what we need to settle on if we want to be in a committed relationship in this century, we can find a way to occupy our time and entertain ourselves. What better way to entertain ourselves than online dating and social media outlets? As singles, we know there's some serious comedy going on in those arenas. Or maybe those outlets have possibly contributed to us being in these desperate situations of revolving door relationships, serial dating, and text affairs. Well, I was trying to lighten things up some, but let's just see where this rabbit hole leads…

Chapter Four:
Online Dating And Social Media: Reality Check-Up

…as I am typing this, I have several notifications beeping on my phone from the umpteen social media apps I have on it. From Facebook to Linkedin to Instagram and my recent excursions into the TikTok world. I currently have my dating apps uninstalled, but I believe my profiles are still up. I think.

Social media and technology itself have added more to the single life scene than I think we know or even understand. I think it has added new mating rituals that go far beyond the bedroom and into cyberspace and somehow make their way into our everyday worlds and interactions. And although we try not to take them seriously and laugh it off, they do influence relationship building or lack thereof. With the onset of internet technology, I will venture to say that another paradigm shift in releationship building between women and men began. The relationship paradigm shift before was the sexual revolution of the 60s, which we will discuss in another chapter. With social media interaction has come new mating rituals that include text and online affairs. When I first became single again after my 10-year relationship/marriage, I did not realize how popular and impactful this ritual was until I was nearly proposed to during a text/online affair.

Well, first, let me explain what a text online affair is for those of you who may not have encountered it yet or may even be in one now but do not know it. A text online affair is mainly where the other person's interactions with you are 95% texting and online. They rarely call you, or you may not have even met the person because they just will not get around to that face-to-face encounter; this is in the case of online buddies or dating online when you haven't met the person. People who text mostly take it very seriously. Well, it's no wonder, as this could be their primary form of human contact. I, for one, prefer talking and the face-to-face. It's difficult for me to take texting and online interactions very seriously. I can't even say it's a generational thing either, as I have met plenty of 40-plus-year-old men online, and all they do is text. I think women are the biggest complainers of text affairs, though. We just like the idea of sharing more and face-to-face interaction because we are more verbal than men, which is why I was flabbergasted when the guy proposed to me during a text; I barely knew his last name, and probably would not have recognized him in a crowd of people from his outdated, blurry pics he shared with me. I think texting is a great tool for men who want to behave badly and women as well. But let's just be honest: there are far more perverted men than women. Debate Me!

Although texting is serious business and shouldn't be underestimated as a tool for relationship building, it's still quite faulty in really getting to know someone. There's just too much that's left out of texting that cannot give us that real sense of knowing a person. You can learn a lot of information about a person through texting and online, just like reading a book on the Gulf War, but if you were there in the Gulf War, your experience becomes so much more robust and accurate. Same for relationship building, face-to-face experiences allow us to build memories with people that enhance the concept of knowing a person tenfold than texting and online ever do. I have always said that texting is the reserved and emotionally detached person's godsend. It allows people already maladaptive in their human contact endeavors to hide behind a false sense of contact. It also helps them foster even more of that closed-off and detached reality they may live within. It is very easy to live vicariously in the world of texting and writing. As a writer, I know this very well. We can write anything and express in this form that we may not be able to do face-to-face and verbally with a person. It certainly can have its benefits for this reason. Sometimes, we can say something to someone in a text and online that we have difficulties sharing verbally. Someone can say they love you in a text message, which is acceptable. Though the impact of saying the words, I love you, to someone's face and in person touches them far more deeply. Creating that bond and attachment in a text is just not as far-reaching. It is not as impactful or meaningful as hearing it in person. People still do want to hear a person say these things, and as women, we especially must hear these affirmations. Women are relational beings that dwell on feelings and emotions.

On to sexting, which is a part of texting. I don't think there's anything wrong with sending flirty, sexy pictures if that's what you want to do as an adult person. I may have a pic or two out there in cyberspace or in some stranger's picture collection; who knows? This is why I also believe we need to be careful about sending full nude pics because we do not know who or where they might end up. And then, who knows if that immature guy you were seeing ends up getting upset with you after a breakup and decides to post them up on www.sheisahoe.com somewhere or send them to someone else. I have never shared any more of my body that someone couldn't see me in on a beach or at a pool with a boyfriend. But I still cringe at the thought of being in India

10 years from now and finding a picture of myself posted in some dingy bathroom. I do believe there needs to be stiffer punishments and follow-through from law enforcement agencies. However, when people intentionally release private pictures that were obviously meant only for them, I think this is a form of defamation of character because it's not being used as intended. Now, if "you" are posting these pictures online, on social media sites, and everywhere, then you must be willing to accept whatever consequences you have coming your way.

Our online interactions, from Facebook to Snapchat, to Instagram, and to all the other places we hang out online, engage so much of our time and interactions that we just cannot ignore the impact and the culture that is forming around these outlets of entertainment. And I say entertainment because it's all still steeped in fantasy. Yes, I do believe we can make connections online, but I do not believe they are very deep. But where the slippery slope lies is that we are spending so much time engaged online, and, like the same with texting, I think we are forgetting that true connections require face-to-face relationship building. But it's so much easier to engage people online than in person. It is also much more fun and forgiving, which is why I think we do it. We may get along great with people online but get face-to-face with that same person, and there just may not be anything there to hold you together, or you may even have an adverse reaction to that person and their personality. We need to start asking why we are engaging so much online. Yes, it's fun, and it's a good pass time. Online has its purpose, but is there some overcompensating going on with the use of online media that may reflect in our own personalities? I think we need to ask ourselves if our online dealings may be nurturing a false sense of connection because we may have or be developing a maladaptive way of communicating with other people. I also believe that the online experience is a bit of a fixation of sorts, much like how a smoker develops an oral fixation after years of smoking. The urgings with the need to do something with our hands, mechanical manipulation, and the need for constant stimulation becomes addictive. In essence, we are over stimulating and creating an insatiable appetite for even more online interactions. There's no other place where I feel this sense of anxiety than when I go to the bathroom, sit down, and realize I left my phone. Oh yes, I know I'm not the only one who will stop what I am doing and go fetch my phone first. Ewww.

And speaking of something that ushers in a sense of anxiety, let's get right on into the discussion of online dating. Before I really delve into this segment, I want to clarify that I am a fan of online dating, as I do believe its pros can outweigh the cons "if" used correctly. With that said, we rarely use online dating correctly, and it's become the devil's baby.

Talk about over stimulation. I believe that we are seeing a new addiction forming in our culture, which is of the serial dater. This is a real thing, folks! And this addiction of serial dating is antithetical to building a true relationship and the life of an independent woman who longs for a long-lasting relationship. Serial dating is just that, where you date person after person, thinking you are getting closer to your true match. There is no committing in serial dating. You could possibly get to the point of several dates with one person but can not get to that next step of commitment. You may even get to the point of sexual encounters with that person within a serial dating episode. It makes us think we are making progress from person to person. But in reality, it enhances the failure rate at record numbers that traditional dating does not allow for in opportunities (when you add the online dating element). This can be quite the numbing effect to someone who does really want to find something meaningful. And it is the commitment of phobe's answered prayer. There are a great number of people who do not want to find anything meaningful and serial dating is what they do. Nothing cultivates the making of the douche bag like online dating. Online dating is a cesspool and petri dish for men who do not want to commit and who may be on agendas with women. The nature of online dating can be anonymous, secretive, and provides for many opportunities, and for a man on an agenda, this is a perfect habitat. A habitat for gamers and immaturity, and an atmosphere that is conducive to game playing, which is why, as women, we must turn this around and make online dating work for us, rather than against us. No decent woman who cares about her body and her spirit wants to go from man to man, whether that be getting to the point of sex with that man or just forming an emotional connection for it to end two months later. What a waste of freaking time. But we are finding ourselves in these very situations with men because we are just not being smart and, again, allowing men to set our parameters and definitions for us.

What we must realize is that online dating works well for men in our culture and at this time in history. A time when there is little incentive to want or need to be in a committed relationship with a woman. This time in history fosters the ideal of the immature male who gets to go to Vegas with his buddies, get tattoos, have sex with as many women as he wants, shirk real responsibilities, and somehow his life turns out okay. These are the images that are most prevalent in our culture. It's not a reality, and looks fun, so why not try it. Online dating fits very well into this unrealistic picture and scene. There are all kinds of online dating sites, from finding a friend with benefits to hook-up sex encounters, to tailored dating experts helping you to find the perfect person for you.

Online dating has created a false sense of hope that there are many people just lined up to be with us, and that may very well be true, but the reality is that not many of those people are compatible with us. There may be a lot of fish in the sea, but not a lot of the right fish for us to swim with. If anything, online dating has created in us this concept of waiting for the bigger, better catch. Instead, we are allowing good, compatible people for us to just swim on by because there's possibly something better over there in that pond.

From the picture painted above, why would any red-blooded male settle down with a woman and hear her nagging him about this or that when he can live with roommates in his parent's basement and get all the free sex from the fish swimming by that he finds online? And somehow, women have bought into this line of thinking and agree that this is okay. Boys just being boys, right? Men behaving badly… and so, we lower our standards with these types of men, allow them into our lives, and then our lives are turned upside down. We end up with unwanted pregnancies, possible STDs, multiple children, working two or three jobs to feed and clothe those children, being left alone, and becoming poorer. Oh, this is getting serious!!

Online dating creates more encounters because it allows us to meet more people, and although online dating is not inherently bad, the prevalence of abuse and misuse, lying, cheating, and working agendas becomes more likely. The nature of being online, anonymous, not face-to-face with a person allows for people who are going to do dirt to feel secure and protected to do that dirt. And by the time you do get to that face-to-face, you may be emotionally engaged with the person. Or at least you think you are. I must note here the difference between serial dating and circular dating. Circular dating is meeting new people and having casual (non-sexual dates with men) in hopes of finding one man with whom we can best relate. I believe in circular dating because it allows us not to put all our eggs in the basket of one man too quickly, leading to serial dating, which is often short-term sexual relationships with men. You are just man-hopping with serial dating. Circular dating, you are exploring your options and remaining emotionally grounded. I mention this because people are falsely or shallowly forming relationships very quickly because they start sleeping together too quickly, and as already indicated earlier, it is critical for women to make sound judgments about men early on.

The amount of time we spend on social media and with online dating, if you are a woman or man who engages in these things, we can begin to believe we are forming bonds that bind. It can be the start of a good or great friendship, but the fact remains we just do not know these people. Knowing comes from experiences shared together. People can write and text you anything, but actions are still tried and true, and the only way you can experience someone's actions is through face-to-face encounters. And going back to the text affairs, I didn't really make this point earlier, but a text affair can be steamy, melodramatic, and filled with passion to the point that you can possibly believe you are falling in love with someone. Your feelings are engaged. But our feelings have deceived us more times than we can count, remember? And because people can tell and write us anything, it doesn't mean that it is true and that they can follow through and back up what they are writing to us, whether it be through a text, online messaging. We just do not know this information until we spend time with that person in real 3D time.

Online dating and social media have their perks and serve a purpose; however, we must make efforts to keep ourselves grounded in a sense when using these mediums of entertainment and communications. We cannot allow ourselves to get too emotionally involved in them, and as women who want something meaningful and long-lasting with a man, we must understand that with the online experience, we will have to develop our own weeding-out tools. We just cannot take our interactions at face value; this is impossible online! Even when we move to the offline encounter and in the initial phase of relationship building, we must continue to keep our standards high. This will come under attack because there are so many men online looking to meet their own selfish needs. We must stop being cheap thrill girls by showing all our goods online with boob and butt shots. We can flirt, have fun, and be silly, but we must maintain boundaries and draw lines for men. This behavior attracts a certain type of man. Even if that man is good-looking and looks like he has something going for him, still and yet, he cannot prove this online. It has to be proven to you face-to-face. Do not put all your eggs in the basket of a man you have not met by allowing him to woo you without action. Again, we must remember that action is tried and true. I cannot say this enough times. In my interactions online, I see men claiming women through Facebook interactions, and that woman will even change her relationship status to "in a relationship," even when she hasn't met the man yet! WTH! This saddens me because I understand the plight of the woman who just wants to be loved so badly by her prince. Again, this stuff has been fed to us for a long time; however, we can wake up from fairy tales and still live dreamy lives with more realistic expectations and boundaries. Not every man online, on social media and dating sites, is out to do you harm, but often, that man is just as confused about what it takes to love as we are, and even more so in many cases. Not to mention again, some do have ill intent. When we become too sexual online and advertise sex (yet we are claiming we are not prostitutes), these actions drip in desperation. Desperation to be loved. Desperation to have a man. Desperation for attention.

Speaking of attention, we must also stop getting upset with men when they approach us provocatively when we put all our ass and tits on display. Yes, no woman deserves to be accosted by any man, but again, we need to be smart about these things and be aware of the attention we may be soliciting from the wrong type of men when we have our entire ass out in selfies and other pictures online or even in public. And then later, we wonder why the man just wanted to have sex with us and leave. You attracted that man from a sexual standpoint from the beginning with your tits and ass on display. This is what prostitutes do literally. Some men do not know how to distinguish the two. There is a fine line between being a fabulous sensual woman and advertising sexually. Come on, Sisters! We gotta start understanding this stuff!

Online dating is no different in this aspect than real life; when we display too much of our body through pictures and videos and all the other means of communication, we are setting ourselves up to receive a certain kind of attention. If that is all you want, then continue to do this, but if you want something meaningful, you must show something meaningful about yourself.

I heard a speaker years ago sharing the male's perspective when it comes to a woman and her nude body. The speaker suggested that when a woman displays her body for all to view, the man will always complete the picture in his mind. And my response to that is, make that man work for that picture. Stop being so free. We put value on ourselves in how we carry ourselves. Again, I'm not a prude and like a short skirt as much as the next woman, but there is still a classy way to wear a short skirt where your ass cheeks are not out. I also believe that how a woman carries herself reveals how she views her womanhood. Unfortunately, in our male-dominated society, men get to decide who are the hoes and who are not. And often, that is determined by how you use your vagina. I'm sorry to say this, ladies, but our vaginas precede us in real life and online. Women are viewed as sexual tools by a great many men. News Flash!! Sex with you is their ultimate goal. And there's nothing inherently wrong with that unless there is lying and manipulations involved, along with a plan to smash and dash. When we think of our vagina in an elevated manner, we begin to understand the power of the pussy. We thwart men from telling us there is no value in it. The pussy is the most valuable piece of meat on the planet! Online and offline!

Chapter Five:
Be A Pussy…Protecting Our Assets!

What is the one thing on the planet that women have that men do not and want most desperately? Yep, I knew you would guess it! The title of this book and chapter: Be a Pussy, is the pinnacle that we must absorb to be successful and practical women of the 21st century. And just as I explained briefly in the introduction, what we do with our vaginas changes our lives daily. What we do not do with our vaginas also changes our lives daily.

Envision the Goose and the Golden Egg and how protective she is of it. How she sits proudly atop that egg and dares anyone, bird or human, to come near her. She will strike. This is how we should be about our vaginas, ladies. I know we are these 21st-century women, and we want to sex it up like the men. It's not fair that men get to sex it up, and we are still labeled hoes when we do. This life is not fair, and do you honestly think any douche cares if you sex him up and leave him? Hell, he's banking on it and planning his exit. It's not about playing games but about being smart.

I have always found it fascinating how we describe weak men as Pussies and the term grow some balls to indicate strength. As women, we go along with this, but deep down, we know the truth. The vagina is the strongest muscle on the planet! I marvel, quite often, at the strength of my own muffin at times and all that she has been through. I remember reading a Facebook meme a couple of years ago with a statement from the late Betty White; I'm not sure if she actually said it, but it certainly rings true about how balls are weak in essence, and yet a vagina is strong because it is the sex organ that takes the pounding. A bit crude but certainly true. In a man's world, things are always flipped upside down and in favor of the man, even when it makes absolutely no sense! We all know that there isn't a more fragile object than a pair of "Balls!"

As women, we can raise the sex standard. Point! Blank! Period! I know I am talking about the new millennial woman here, the 21st-century woman. And as much as we want and should be equal to men, we are still not in many arenas. And sex is the primary one. I know many women think that if they are to knock down this proverbial wall of unfairness, we must somehow become more like men, especially in our sexing. That we must expose ourselves and have as many partners as the man, and we should not be unfairly scrutinized for this. And yes, we should not be, but the reality is that we are indeed unfairly scrutinized. Not how we think we are being treated unfairly, though. Nowadays, it is being nurtured in the media mainly that a woman should have sex like a man and hit as many partners as she can without a second thought. That she is being elevated as some kind of independent, free-thinking woman when she does. This is male benefits package 101: How to marginalize women through sex. Women are still being labeled as loose and getting sexed up by as many men as they allow to run through them. It's unfair because the game isn't fair. Men are holding more cards than we are. And we are playing by their rules. One of the biggest tricks of an oppressive system is getting people to participate in their own oppression, as I have mentioned in previous chapters. We are still coming out on the short end of the stick, again with unwanted pregnancies, STDs, financial shortfalls, heartbreaks, etc.

Because as much as some women like to say they can be just as hard as a man and can suppress emotions when it comes to sex and relationships, we still struggle with wanting love and to be loved by the man to whom we are giving our bodies and emotions. Plus, men have us beat on the getting hard part; it's their nature or something like that.

It's more in our nature as women to want love, care, and adoration. Of course, a male-dominated society will always nurture the idea of women giving up their bodies to them with no consequences. Again, that's in their favor. Men are highly sexual beings and even more so in the perversion of sex. Women are just as sexual but not as perverted, but somehow, we have been falsely labeled as not sexual enough. Male-dominant culture cultivates a systematic control of a woman's sexuality that always plays out to a man's benefit. But giving in to those social and behavioral controls is not where we want to be. It is reverse psychology at its best. Sexing up men like men is playing right into a sex-crazed society where men continue to control us through our sexuality and our vaginas.

We must control our own vaginas. I'm ready to have a Million Pussy March on Washington yesterday. As single women, especially, we can decide to put a lockdown on our pussies until we figure out how we want to utilize them. The late and great Prince said it best when he sang "Pussy Control." We must realize the power that we hold between our legs. We are life bearers and carriers. Portals to this consciousness from possibly somewhere else that none of us knows about. We deserve more respect than we are given and must demand it for ourselves. We are WOMBman, and our wombs must be held in high esteem by us, first and foremost.

Men are using our vaginas as currency, and we also do to a certain degree and should, as it is ours to use! Men get quite upset when we mention this and that our vaginas belong to us, and we will use them as we see fit. But we are missing the point in using them most efficiently and not having our vaginas work for us but against us in many cases. Many men are surely gaining more from the deal than we are, and when I refer to guys, men in this case, I am talking about douchebags and no good as men. Because a real man, a good man, and a true Champion man, understand the value of a woman and her vagina and that her muffin will carry his seed and nurture his children. A douche can care less; he does not see a woman in this light. He literally sees women as walking pussy and how many he can collect. And if he has collected many, then he feels like the testosteroney manly man we seem to encounter all too often these days! Now, the no-good-ass man wants to annihilate your vagina because he is a woman hater. So, you are damn straight; we must protect ourselves and understand we hold the power with our vaginas and must control our vaginas. We must bring our own vaginas under subjugation to what we want for her. It is us, ladies, who create these dogs in men by what we are so freely giving to them. We are creating the very men who are abusing us. Sexing us and leaving us.

Nothing broke my heart more in my field of work in social services than when I would encounter young, poor women with a house full of children and no man in sight. The biggest asset a poor woman has is her vagina and what she does with it. What she does with her vagina can take her places or leave her stuck. It's no secret or judgment that the more children a poor person has out of wedlock (male or female) and with no partners to help, the poorer that person is and becomes.

The reality is children are expensive, dammit! The mother usually stays with her children she bears if there is a breakup, taking care of that man's bad-ass seeds. The woman can get stuck in a life of food stamps, low-income housing, and other various government supplements to help subsidize the lack and absence of that father.

I once was a woman living in similar circumstances when I got pregnant during my freshmen year in college. Thank God I took a hint and put a clamp down on my coochie! I only have one child to date. But back then, I lived in low-income housing, was on food stamps, and received cash benefits from the state for some time. Something told me to stay in school, and I did; that was one of my tickets out, and I graduated. And thankfully, my son's dad was always in his life, even though we weren't together. It was one of the rare cases where the guy took care of his child as well. This is critical for you and your child(ren), but there are no guarantees that man will stick around and help you and his child, which is where being smart comes in.

Giving ourselves to a man so quickly and sexing with him while we don't know if he will commit to us and our children in case we become pregnant should be a constant thought of precaution. We have too much to lose, ladies if we continue to be dumb on this issue. Our children are suffering! It shouldn't take four childbirths to come to this realization. This is harsh, but it must be said and heard. In my line of work, I know women are doing the best they can, but you cannot get upset with the man (or men) because you don't know him (them). Yes, there are some lying, cheating men out here who take advantage of women, which is my point. Protect our interests and stop looking for a man to save and complete us.

We are losing out; we are on the brink of emotional and mental breakdowns; we are struggling with our finances; we are overwhelmed caring for multiple children by ourselves, having panic attacks, can't make ends meet, angry and bitter because of the situations we find ourselves in. All because we believed a lie that somehow a man would save us. I am there with you ladies. I have believed this lie for years. I have been all of the above with the exception of multiple children. One child is hard enough. I almost can't imagine the struggle with more. But it gives me insight into how difficult it has to be to get out of situations like this when there are even more children to care for. We have to wizen up, be smart, and stop being dumbass like the cashier in chapter one and shortchanging ourselves. We are literally not protecting our ASSets and giving up the ass too quickly and to the wrong men. There is work to be done. Later in this book, I hope to help identify some of these wrong men and their characteristics so we can avoid them altogether.

If you are a woman and mother in the situation mentioned above, doing the best you can, know that you are a good person. Although your sanity is hanging on at the end of the thread, your children are fed, they are clean, they are getting an education, and their needs are being met. You, too, can wizen, wake up and stop putting so much faith in a man. Take control of your life and your vagina by setting some goals to help get yourself out of these situations, not just for yourself but for your children, while that baby's daddy may be tip-toeing down the street to Susie Q. Dumbass's house and making more babies. It's time to wake up!

This is how bad it's gotten. These MFers are making songs about mistreating us, sexing, and leaving us, and we are dancing to these songs. I'm guilty, too. I listen to those songs, and I'm like, what the hell in my mind and still dancing! Again, having us participate in our own oppression. If we don't control our own pussies, men will, and they are telling us how they are going to do it. Gotta love their confidence. Why do we think this stuff is so prevalent around us? These misogynistic songs on the radio waves? Our children are even bobbing their heads to it; we're singing it with them. Oh, it's no big deal; it's just a song. I don't know about you, but there are songs that have literally changed my life and helped me make decisions in my life. There is more to this. It is a system. A reaction to a response. A system that is designed to oppress and slight. It all does have meaning. Nothing is meaningless. Even mindless chatter serves a purpose. Maybe what I'm saying now is mindless chatter to some. But I do know that there are far more women who can relate to the above than those who can not. Too many who can, and I'm also sure some women cannot. But as a woman, I feel it's my place to help my fellow sisters. Sisters who either don't know any better, or who have engaged in bad decision making, or ones that just got blindsided by a lying ass man. Whatever the reason or however, we have gotten to a certain place that is far less, only to realize we are there and plan to change and make better decisions from here. This is where I am, ladies, right now as I write these words to you. I am so ready to take control of my life, my vagina, and all that belongs to Miriam. Sign me up for that 20 million pussy march on Washington. I think, as women, we must be ready to start a revolution of sorts. Take our vaginas back and start defining what we want as women from the men we enter relationships with.

Not all of this is social and cultural; some of it is physiological and biological. There is something natural placed in our feminine makeup that once we start engaging in sexual intercourse with a man, we basically lose our minds in a sense. Especially when we start relying on our emotionally reactive brain side to make our decisions for us. It's called Oxytocin, and I will detail this little-known hormone in a later chapter. But our emotions get us in trouble with men all the time. In how we were designed, sex and our emotions are directly linked. All of you strong-minded women who will disagree with me on this, I would like a public list of all the men you have dated and screwed. And please provide their phone numbers so that I can call them and ask them about your emotional level and if you became a crazed bitch at some point. Yeah, like I thought!

I do not mean to suggest that being the emotional creatures that we were created to be is a bad thing, but because things have changed so much with men, and the definitions of relationships have changed, our emotions once linked to sex with a man can be counterproductive and obsolete at times. Ladies, we need to upgrade to something that works better. This is why I am making the following upgrade suggestion:

- The free vagina buffet is now closed. All you can eat, and ala cart is no more.

- Contracts are in full effect mode now.

For starters, I challenge all women who are not in a marriage bond or committed relationship to close shop and close the coochie buffet for 30 days. Let's just pick a day to start together and choose not to have sexual intercourse for at least 30 days. If you are a woman who wants more from your mate, a commitment, a family, a future with one man in your life, this is my suggestion to you. I challenge you to do this. You must make a point and make it loud and clear to that man. You can blame me if you like and if you are unhappy with the "sleeping arrangement" you have right now and are going nowhere. And believe me, if that man has not committed to you yet, that is all that you have. You have to be ready to risk losing that man, and you will have to live with that. In my opinion, if you lose him, you never had him in the beginning. And the fact that you are considering such a drastic point-making tool, then you do not have that man. I'm just helping you to see this. The fact that you are willing to lose the man also takes out the game playing that some will perceive this to be. Choosing not to have sex with a man or stopping sex with a man who will not commit to you is not game-playing. It is you saying things are not working as they stand right now. Your needs and wants are not being met, and you need to take time for yourself to reflect on what it is you want. It is time to clear your mind without your emotions being so tossed and turned with the sexual element there for further influence.

The fact that this is not game-playing is the very reason why I don't advocate for women in marriage and committed relationships to do this. I feel that if you are married or in a committed relationship and withhold sex or have stopped having sex with your mate, then you are playing games with them. Why are you still with this man if you are doing this or want to stop having sex with them? If these things are going on within the confines of commitment, that commitment has already been broken, and a possible separation is in order. A physical separation is in order, as you are already emotionally separated if you stop having sex. Again, this is not game-playing. Game-playing is when you are not serious about losing someone or being alone. You just want to punish them. This is not about punishment. Taking control of your vagina, clearing your thought processing on what you want in your life and from a partner is about you. It also sends a clear message to the person you are sleeping with, which, again, we have established is all you are doing. It sends the message to them that something is wrong, off, and if they cannot meet some of your requirements, they too need to decide if they want to stay and work out a satisfactory plan with you or leave.

To truly be that independent woman who understands her worth and who will define for herself what she wants and not continue to take cues from a male-dominant society that is becoming more non-conducive to what is productive, moral, and right for us as women, we must be willing to be alone or left by a man.

A great example of how women take cues from their environment and place them onto their lives even at their own detriment comes from a fantastic movie, The Color Purple. Whoopi Goldberg's character, Celie, was a battered and abused woman; she was certainly oppressed while living with Mister. In the scene where Harpo is trying to figure out a way to control his wife Sophia, Celie tells Harpo to "Beat her." Now, why would anyone who has lived under such oppression tell someone to oppress another with the same? As human beings, we tend to respond to what we know rather than what may be right. As women, we do this all the time. We know in our heart of hearts that giving our body so quickly to a man may result in us being used and left, and then we are heartbroken. But society and culture tell us that we have to have sex with a man, and quickly, in order to keep him or grab him. Well, I don't know about you; that ain't and hasn't worked for me. So, why do we continue to do this? Because we are blindly responding to those cues without critically thinking. We are defining by definitions that have been given to us. And even using outdated definitions that are not even in effect anymore for where our culture is on male/female relations.

Firstly, we need to understand that our definitions and defining cannot be flimsy and see-through. They must be based off the building blocks of what strong, committed relationships stand upon. Come up with bullshit definitions, and you will continue to get bullshit. I have seen those lists women have that don't even make any sense. I have made my own even. Now, I look back on that crap, and it's no wonder I was attracting crapola men! Thankfully, I wasn't entertaining them for long; at least, I had that much sense.

Communication with that man in your life or with any future men who come into your life and what your requirements are is critical. And if they cannot reciprocate, that is not the man for you. It is up to us to self-define, share, and stick by our convictions. Again, no bullshit definitions, where as soon as a man smiles at us, we forget about our boundaries. Some women have gone so far out in the left field that they bought the lie they are not supposed to have any requirements in their life or from men. They are "that" afraid of not having a man with them.

Your definitions should build around the concepts of respect levels, communication, fidelity, trust, security, etc. And be specific when sharing them with that man:

- "In order for me to feel secure in this relationship, I need you to stop flirting with other women, stop giving your undivided attention to other women, and reserve that attention for me."

- "In order for me to feel respected by you, I need for you to not put me down in public and at home, not use me as the brunt of your jokes."

- "In order for me to feel like I'm a priority in your life, I need you to come home after work instead of going straight to the bar to meet up with your friends."

- "In order to feel like I am moving forward in this relationship, I need for us to sit down periodically and discuss our future plans with each other."

Those questions and your definitions need to be discussed early on and/or they need to be brought up in the relationship at some point, and give that man an opportunity to answer the question. Make sure he answers the questions and your definitions. Be calm, direct, and kind in your delivery because there is no need to get bent out of shape when you are asking or sharing with someone you love. Any man who says he loves you and wants to be in your life should have no problem discussing this with you and answering your questions. You may need to give him a little bit of time within reason, as some men just process things slower, and any emotionally stable man would have no qualms in discussing the above, again, as long as it's brought in a constructive, calm manner. Your definitions need to be specific to what you want and need to thrive in a relationship with a man. If that man is not emotionally stable, you will know by his reactions to this. And watch his reactions! This is where taking your time with a man must come into place if it is the beginning of a relationship. With a man you are getting to know, you must define your boundaries along the lines of the above very early on.

- "I do not allow a man to my home on the first date."

- "I am celibate until I marry."

- "I will not sleep in the same bed with you until I am comfortable that you have my best interests in mind."

- "I will not have sex with you until I know and you have proven to me you want more from me."

Again, if that man is emotionally stable, he will work with you and build a better relationship. And if it's the beginning of a relationship and that man wants more from you, he will stick around. Be vigilant, though. Don't fall into the "Oh, he must like me; he bought me something" or "He must really be into me because he texts me every day," then drop your guard, and all your definitions go down the toilet. Some men are very good at keeping up a façade for a long time. If that man becomes withdrawn, belligerent, or passive-aggressive about any of this, again, this is not the man for you and ladies… Drop him!! Stop dating someone's potential. I tried to live with a man who was just not emotionally stable, and everything I brought to him was taken as an affront and an attempt to control him. There is always room for discussion and compromise. We should be willing to work with a person, but if it becomes a running theme that they shut down every time you bring something up or you can't talk without fighting, then again, that man is quite possibly not for you. But even with the above examples, none of this is too much to ask a man with whom you are in a committed relationship.

We have lost sight of what it means to be in a loving relationship with someone. We want to help our partners and do the things to help them to be happy. Again, we want to accommodate them within reason and make their lives easier and more productive for them. By doing so, our own lives become more enriched. The immaturity that is so prevalent these days says that the above is too much to ask and that it is okay for the other person to lash out at you for being reasonable and wanting something deeper, more meaningful, and lasting. It still amazes me how far we have gotten from mutual respect. I blame much of this on media and television, which are feeding us some of the worst of the worst when it comes to relationship building and what that looks like. I encourage people to turn off these reality shows and sitcoms because they are poison to the mind and have a greater influence on us than we think.

I know for me; I want to think more critically about what is going on in this single scene I have found myself in on and off over the last 15 years. Self-defining and taking note of what I want is a must. We cannot afford to approach relationships haphazardly anymore. Check the box Yes, and we are dating; we are together… those days are long gone. I remember 25 years ago when it seemed easier to find a man who wanted a committed and monogamous relationship, or maybe it was my age or both, and some other things playing a factor in how I related to men. What I do know is that much has changed in 25 years, both in society and within myself. Women have changed, and so have men.

Along with self-defining, we also contend with other aspects that we must grasp if we are to be successful or start feeling fulfilled within a loving relationship with a man. Understanding what we are dealing with when it comes to the men we are encountering today is a huge factor. What the hell are we working with here? Who are the bad guys, and who are the good ones? I don't know about you, but I didn't get the memo on this, and believe me, ladies, there is a memo on this shit, for real!! I suggest you find it, read it, and learn it. In the following chapter, I hope to bring some light to recognizing certain character types in men. So not only do we have to self-define for ourselves, but we have to self-define with the knowledge of what options we have in men or who we are attracting into our lives. We must learn men and how they operate in today's culture, so that we are not blindly responding to the cues that keep us unhappy and unfulfilled.

Chapter Six:
Douche Bags, No Good Ass Men, And The Walking Wounded: Season 2

Okay, ladies, shit is about to get real real in this chapter. This is the chapter where we collaborate on some thangs. This is a work in progress, even for myself, as I'm trying to figure out what is going on with men in our society. I'm still looking for the missing memo on this topic, so bear with me. However, I do hope to arrive at some conclusions about what's going on in American Singledom. What I do know, without a doubt, is we have to recognize what and who a "Good" man is. To do that, we must also learn what the bad ones look like. I will attempt to help us tell them apart.

Again, if you are like me and going into the second half of your life, season 2, 30s and beyond, you start to realize you have to get this shit right! I have developed three categories of men for myself. There could be more, which I'm pretty sure there are. My categories are:

- The "Douche Bag," DB for short

- The "No Good Ass Man," NGAM for short, and then there is:

- The average Good Guy, who we will term the "Walking Wounded," WW for short

I have already used some of these terms throughout this book for certain men, and there may not have been a clear and distinct difference. Or, at times, I may have used them interchangeably and loosely, blending one into the other. But make no mistake, ladies, there are distinct differences in these types of men; recognizing them is critical to our survival in this single and dating scene of the 21st century. C'mon, ladies, we are multitasking royalty. We cannot get lazy now when it comes to the men we are dating, seeing, and allowing into our lives. This laziness is part of the problem. I largely think because we have been allowing men to make these critical decisions for us, and as we have determined, many men do not want this job duty any longer and are in an all-in-out rejection mode of it.

Firstly, I will provide my definitions of each of these types of men. These definitions are based mostly on my firsthand experiences and shared experiences by other single women I know or stories from other women shared with me who may or may not be single now. As you have probably guessed, the definitions can be quite subjective. Again, this is my book, and I'm running things in here. Remember me, the control freak! Anywho, I know many ladies will agree with most of my definitions and can relate. Secondly, I will then list the general character traits, mannerisms, and behaviors of each type of man and what we need to look for in each. And since I am somewhat a fair person and because these definitions and character traits can be so individualized, I have left lines after my definitions and list for you to enter your own definitions and character traits based on your own personal experiences.

Yall ready? Hold on tight! This one is a ride, for sure. `

First up is the **Douche Bag**, **DB**.

Before we delve into the Douche, we have to break down the term douche itself first. It is a male or possibly female-created term that took off in movies in the 1980s especially. Back then, it meant an arrogant azzhold of a man. Of course, as women, we know what a real douche is that helps with hygiene. Well, the Douchebag man can literally aide in why you may need a douche after dealing with him. Okay… REAL REAL! To describe the DB, he is a man who is known to the world around him as a douchebag. This man may even tell you he is a DB. The Douche makes no apologies for being a douche. Most Douches are very charismatic, funny, and are typically ladies' men. This man is also very likely to give you an STD if you have unprotected sex with him because of his reckless nature. They love swishing around in women's vaginas. But this is also the thing about a Douche that differentiates him; he is a Douche for a season. Once a DB, not necessarily always a DB. The DB is a man who wants to lick you up and down until you say stop…if you know that was a song lyric, you are probably a '70s & '80s kid. But I digress.

A Douche is not trying to settle down. He is not looking for a girlfriend currently in this reality we are in! But he will sweep you off your feet like no other and move very quickly with you. A Douche will tell you very early on that he "loves you." A DB will have several women he is seeing and sexing. He may be stretching the truth with some dumb women who believe he is their boyfriend. But he is caught in lies quite a bit because he doesn't really care or want to be in a relationship with just one woman anyway. He is banking on you catching him up in a lie so that you can leave him alone, and he can move on smoothly to the next victim. Most DB's get away with being a DB so often because they are typically easy on the eyes, and some women believe they can tame the Douche. I will say this: if it is fantastic sex that you want from a man, the DB is your guy because he is a freak. But, make no mistakes; that is all you will get from him.

Now, I mentioned that a DB is often a Douche for a season. A Douche can be reformed and will reform himself when he is ready to settle down. Don't ever think that you can settle this man down by doing something on your end. You will never be pretty enough, you will never be a good enough cook, and you will never be able to care for him enough to stop him from being a Douche. All you will be in the end is hurt if you try. At times, you may even see some morals that peek out in a douche which is why he can be so deceiving. The DB is that man who will text you to check up on you after he has cheated on you if you were Susie Q. Dumbass enough to think he was your boyfriend from the beginning. In his mind, he is genuinely checking up on you because "he misses you," "you are different," "make him feel a certain way." But mostly, he's just keeping you around to be on his weekly booty call roll.

Quite often, the Douche can be perceived as a Savior of women, of sorts. He can be quite passionate and even fight and brawl for any woman he is sexing at the time. This, too, can be confusing for the women he is sexing. He may have jealous fits with any of these women because he can be possessive, even though he will not like you for trying to put him on "lockdown" and will probably use those very words. The Douche Bag loves drama and will quite often have many female "friends" who may also be vehement defenders of him and creates a scene of drama swirling around him.

The DB's phone constantly goes off with text messages and other alerts at all times of the night because he's such a wanted man. This man must be needed by people and women, which is why he is so good at being a Douche. A DB is the same man who will try sexting with you as soon as you meet him or want to dirty talk with you on your first conversation because nothing is sacred with him. He does this with every woman. A DB likes the risk of it all, the risk of being caught, chasing women, sexing her, and then doing his own thing. Mainly because he can and that he is simply an immature male who doesn't appreciate the benefits of a relationship right now. The DB may party often and hang out at bars and clubs. Some DBs are quieter or have quiet noise type of drama but will still have most of the above going on at any given time. Some DBs are jobless or in dead-end jobs with no careers. Immaturity seems to span across a person's life, and for most DBs, you can see this not just in their relationships but in everything they do.

This man is not a harmless man. He preys on weak-minded women, the ones with low self-esteem, whom he gravitates towards. He will have you up all night crying over him and will offer to come over and comfort you. That went well the last time, right? The DB has no intentions of changing until he is ready. The signs will be there. They will be clear, and for the most part, the Douche is not about hiding them. Which, again, can be a bit endearing to women. We will even say things like, "he didn't lie about anything," or "he was upfront," which admitting to willingly being a dumbass is the first step to recovery. I'm just being honest. Don't get it twisted, though, the Douche can care less if you get him or not. He gets bored very easily and must have a new girl regularly because he is like a child. When one toy gets old, he simply throws it on the floor and finds a new one. He may come back and play with that old toy later, but he is always on the hunt for a new toy. A DB is known for staying in contact with his exes because he's just that charming.

A Douche can serve a purpose if you, too, are not looking for a relationship. But just know, lady, that as a woman, you will never be able to compartmentalize like a male Douche. And you really shouldn't want to. This type of person uses people and discards them for whatever reasons; he's hurting, commitment issues, mommy issues, who knows! A Douche is a user of women because he is emotionally crippled and immature and has no idea how to maintain longevity in a relationship, and most importantly, the DB doesn't really care to know at this point in his life. This is why he can also reform himself later in life by just growing up and having some experiences to help him mature.

Okay, here is a list of Characteristics to look for when encountering a Douche:

1. Charming
2. Only looking for friends with benefits (sexing and leaving you), A Douche may even reveal early on that he wants sex
3. Charismatic, passionate (which is why so many women fall for him)
4. Immature: may get into fights over you (don't be impressed)
5. Has many female friends
6. Handsome, nice body (works out at the gym a lot because he may not have a job)
7. Self-centered

8. Cocky
9. Always has drama going on (social media whore)
10. Is a partier
11. Is known as a Douche by other women
12. Can be Reformed when he's ready and only when he's ready (don't think YOU can reform him)
13. May not hold a job long
14. Has roommates and over the age of 30 years old.
15. May have a couple of Baby mamas
16. Drinks excessively
17. Has peekaboo moral flashes here and there
18. Will try to stay in contact with you with no real reason to do so (other than getting some booty from you)
19. Upon first contact, he will try to sext with you and try to pull you in on dirty talk with him (to make you his cheap thrill girl)

Now, please write down some of your definitions of what you believe a Douche Bag man is to you that may be different than mine above.

_____

_____

_____

_____

_____

_____

_____

_____

_____

_____

_____

_____

_____

_____

_____

_____

_____

_____

_____

_____

<u>List some character traits you have experienced from a man you believed to be a DB male.</u>

1._____

2._____

3._____

4._____

5._____

My next attempt will be to define what I like to call just an ordinary man, a good man but a "Walking Wounded" WW of a man. This man is in his 30s-50s. Before I go on, I must remind you that we have pretty much established that the Champion Man, although does exist, you have a slim to no chance, at this point in the game, to encounter him in the wild. That champion man most likely has been captured and tamed by his queen, his goddess, his soulmate, and he and she are living happily ever after. Again, if you would like, you can wait on this rare find; you can set up all the traps you think you may need to capture him. Good luck with that; I do wish you the best.

Now, if you would like to join the rest of us steeped in reality, I will share some good news. This is the thing about just an ordinary man, a good man who is the Walking Wounded… it is quite possible that at one point in time, this WW of a man was a Champion man. Life may have gotten the best of him, he couldn't live up to so many demands and expectations, and he may have encountered just a no-good-ass woman (yes, they are out there too) who mistreated him, hence why he is the Walking Wounded. Now, with this said, because of these champion traits that were once inside him, he has a good chance of morphing into your champion man again. Not a high probability, but it's quite possible. Also, even if he was never a Champion man, he could possibly still become your Champion man, given he is willing to work on himself and allow you to help him.

But I have to say this: it is not your job to force this man into becoming what you think he should be. He has been bruised and badgered enough. He is the Walking Wounded; this man, instead, will need you to help him mend some. The WW requires a lot of patience, love, and care. He will be a good man to you regardless of if he has that shining medal of a champion. So, you must ask yourself if what this man is offering is enough for you, and this is where I would insert: don't be a greedy heifer! The WW must be accepted for what he is. He will have baggage, to say the least. But a good man will always allow you to help him unpack, and he will help you unpack yours as well. The WW is a workable man. But he may be limping; he may not see clearly out of one eye; he may even be a little gun shy about committing too soon, but he wants to be in a relationship, unlike Douche. WW men are made for relationships and actually do quite poorly when not in them. The WW has probably been in several failed relationships and/or very long-term relationships 10-20 years that have come to its demise.

Never enter a relationship (sexual) with a WW who is freshly out of a relationship. This man rebounds women like nobody's business. Because, again, he wants to be in a relationship. Wait at least a year if he has been in a long-term relationship (5-20 years) or six months to a year with a shorter-term relationship. He will most likely be honest with you about his last one. This is why WW man sometimes remains in the state of WW because he does go from relationship to relationship so quickly. But his intentions are good. If this man would do some work on himself, he could and often becomes a great man. Even once he is in a relationship with you, he will still require a lot of emotional support and work on himself. For the reason of his rebounding issues, DO NOT JUMP INTO BED WITH THIS MAN TOO QUICKLY!! I cannot stress this enough. Thankfully, the Walking Wounded man will most likely have a moral compass of sorts and can be honest with you. But he is still a man. He may even go to church and have a spiritual life. In my opinion, a man with a spiritual life is the most workable because he has allowed an outside/inside source of accountability to influence his life. Men who do not have that spirituality are like an island unto themselves, and those men can be the toughest men to live with because they are without accountability and no anchor. They set the rules, and although there is nothing innately wrong with this, if that man has not worked through issues, he can be tough to make changes or amendments in his life. This is a personal question you need to ask yourself on your, what's important scale. Not jumping into bed with the WW gives you a chance to feel him out, know where he is in life, and if he is the man for you. If you want a strong commitment from this man, you have to give him and yourself time. I'm not going to set any formulas or timeframes; however, I will say this: give it a few months. A good man will not mind waiting, and if he doesn't want to wait, then you know he is a waste of your time and most likely a Douche in disguise. Come on, ladies, we have been down this road too many times not to know this.

The WW will most likely work, have a job, and even have a career. He most likely will have his own place with no roommates. If he does not have his own place, it could be due to a recent divorce or a big change in his life, but this man rarely stays with others for long, whether it is family or friends. He will have a plan. This man will have goals in life and, for the most part, follow through on them, and you will be able to see some of his results. This is the man you can have a long-term relationship with. He has a high commitment level and has most likely been in longer-term relationships before yours of 5 years or more.

Physically, the WW will be average to good-looking. He can possibly be overlooked by some women who are just not paying attention. You should, will, and can have a sexual spark with him or chemistry. Your sex life will be average to great, maybe below average at times, depending on what's going on with him, as he can be moody. He may have some financial issues from divorce and child support. You probably don't want to merge your finances with the WW. I'm not a big proponent of merging finances with another person. You can still foster financial success and support your partner without merging your finances. Now, marriage requires a different type of financial divisions and compartments.

The Walking Wounded Man will be attentive to you because he wants to be with you, and you have given him and yourself that time to be sure. This man can appreciate this. This man has a high propensity to be faithful and loyal if he is not freshly out of a relationship, as mentioned. When the WW is fresh out of a relationship and is not giving himself time and working on himself, he can be as dangerous as a Douche. He is like a fish out of water when not in a relationship if he is not consciously working on himself. He makes very poor decisions after a breakup. It is not unusual to see a WW man in his 40s with a two-year-old on his hip because he thought he was in love with a 25-year-old. Again, run the opposite direction if a WW man approaches you and he has only been single for a month or so. A WW can look like a DB for a brief period when he is on a bad decision roll. Tell him to do some work on himself and get himself together, and if he wants to seek you out after that, you will be more than happy to chat with him. But until then, NO!

After a WW man has worked on himself as best that he knows how, and is ready to seek you out, give yourself that time and allow his actions to line up with his words. The thing about the WW is that he is a good man and will treat you well and will work with your children if you have any. This man loves the idea of family and being part of a family. Again, take that time before you even do introductions with your children to ensure this is the man you want around your children. This man will even go to counseling with you if you want him to. He may not get much out of it, but the efforts will be there. He may be argumentative at times, but give him his space.

The WW male will be somewhat affectionate but could range to very affectionate. He will show his love for you by his actions and may be able to tell you on occasion that he loves you. He may not be a very emotional man at all, which is ideal for me; I don't want an emotional man whining as much as I do. But to each their own. He can be romantic at times, which can also range up or down by personality. The WW is not the fairytale prince of our dreams, but if given a chance, he will love us very deeply. And he can be a friend to us. To love a WW male, a woman must be mature herself. There must be an acceptance of this man if you are to find happiness with him. When in a relationship with a WW man, a woman must have her own interests and things she does. This is not a man who is going to wrap his whole life around you, and I question how healthy that is anyway. He will support you; however, he is not going to be at your beck and call to do everything you want him to do. And having your own interests and hobbies will help you not to be so wrapped up in him all the time. The really good news about the average, everyday WW man is there are still many of these in the general population than any other man.

Okay, here is a list of Characteristics to look for when encountering a Walking Wounded man:

1. Average
2. Good man (by your definitions you have)
3. Wants to be in a relationship and shows this to you
4. Confused at times
5. Financial issues
6. Dependable within a committed relationship
7. Works and has a steady job
8. Responsible (you can see this in his life)
9. Have a moral compass, spiritual life
10. May have younger children (brain fart with a younger woman)

11. Most likely will have older, possibly grown children whom he has a good relationship with
12. Is workable and will allow you to help him some
13. Can morph into a champion man, if he does a lot of emotional work on himself
14. Is the rebound king because he wants to be in a relationship so badly...avoid him during his rebound period
15. Once in a committed relationship with you, he will help you with your children if you have any
16. Good, fair, possibly great sex life.
17. May have a flash of Doucheness (mainly when fresh out of a relationship when he makes his poorest decisions).
18. Has the best potential to be a long-term partner and healthy mate for life

Now, please write down some of your definitions of what you believe a Walking Wounded, Average man is to you that may be different than mine above.

_____

_____

_____

_____

_____

_____

_____

_____

_____

_____

_____

_____

_____
_____
_____
_____
_____
_____
_____
_____

List some character traits you have experienced from a man you believed to be a WW man.

1._____

2._____

3._____

4._____

5._____

I wanted to save the Devil for last. The No-Good Ass man, better known as NGAM. AKA...the devil incarnate. The No-Good Ass Man is not fit to be a man to any woman. This man is a woman hater. He is a predator to women and a parasite who will try to steal, kill, and destroy the spirit of a woman. You would think a man like this would be easy to see, much like the douche. Oh no, quite the opposite. This man is the devil, as I have stated. He literally transforms himself as it suits him, which is the danger of this man. He will appear to be your champion man, but make no mistakes; he is a wolf in sheep's clothing. The NGAM is not sloppy like the Douche. He is way too sophisticated for that tomfoolery.

The NGAM is a very manipulative man. He is very intelligent and calculating and will most likely be very secretive, but he will term this as being private. This male will be a womanizer; however, you will never know this because he is so secretive and discreet in most things he does. He can put on the appearance and even be presented as a pillar in his community, but behind closed doors, this man is a tyrant. He is controlling, and any woman he is with will be under his reign of control. This is his goal. Thankfully, your stint with this man as an independent woman will be short because you just will not stick around with him, and he will not tolerate you for too long as you are just too aggressive of a woman for him. He may even call you this at some point, and he hates everything about you as an independent woman, which is the very reason he comes after you at all: He loves to break down a woman. You are just a challenge for him, but his interests do not go beyond that. This man's real pursuit is a passive woman lacking self-esteem who will hopefully stay with him for a long time. And unfortunately, this woman's spirit will be broken by the time he finishes with her. She will rarely leave him and if she does, it may be thanks to a good support system of friends and family who will assist her in getting out of his grip.

Because this man can do serious harm to a woman physically, mentally, spiritually, and emotionally, it is critical to recognize the No-Good Ass Man early on. Things to look for in the NGAM early on is that he will move fast with you. Like stated above, he will appear to be your Champion man. He looks like the prince from the fairytale you have dreamed of. Like the Douche, this man will also sweep you off your feet. He will be very materialistic and show off his toys to you and possibly even shower you with gifts, jewelry, vacations, and his attentions very early on. He can possibly be quite standoffish and reserved, which we can misinterpret as mysterious. He will most likely have a very good job and some independence with his wealth. The NGAM is driven professionally because he knows the power that money and material things can have, and he loves using it manipulatively. You may think in your mind or say to others that you feel like you are in a dream with him or think this is too good to be true. You best believe it honey… It is!

As you get to know the NGAM, he is quite arrogant. His sense of humor is typically dry and void. This man may not have many friends and has cut off relationships, possibly with family and his children, because he lacks a real emotional connection with people in general. Even if he has any children, it is a manipulative relationship where he must hold all the cards, and he may possibly even use his wealth to manipulate his own children.

The NGAM will most likely be OCD; his home will be impeccable and, if not impeccable, way too clean, orderly, and put together for an average man. Pay attention, ladies. This is part of his controlling ways, and don't you try to move anything or do anything in his home contrary to what he does; he will be quick to change it back or move it to its rightful place. This could be a test on your part to see how controlling he is; just move something or do something different from how he does it, and you will see. Now, normally, as women, we do this. Right! As women, we love things in their rightful place, a clean house, etc. This is a feminine trait. And that's not to say men cannot be clean and organized because they can and still be good men. But the

NGAM will take this to the next level, almost into a feminine energy. Most average men don't fret about household things like that.

The NGAM is quite defensive, over-analytical, and paranoid in his thinking of others, which is where he will start in on you. This man has a skewed sense of reality. He is most likely not a spiritual man and an island unto himself. He makes the rules, so accountability with him is not likely. Once this man knows he has you, he will start to pick you to shreds.

Now, for the independent woman, this targeting from him will come suddenly. But for the woman he has in his grips, he will do this over time and enjoy her breakdown for possibly years. He will tell you what to wear, what color is your favorite color, how often you should go to the gym, and what you should eat for dinner. For a woman not paying attention, this may come off as possessiveness, or he just wants the best for you. He will want you all to himself; if you have children, they will not be included in too many of your activities with this man, if at all. Again, if he has children, he will probably only have one, maybe two children. He has always looked at children as an inconvenience for him. He is a very selfish man. The NGAM does not pay too many compliments to any woman outside of the beginning of a relationship with him. In the beginning, he may be very complimentary, but, again, if you are paying attention, the compliments will wane off. Instead, it will be replaced with critical remarks about and towards you. He is a jealous man, mainly of you, your family, friends, and other relationships. The NGAM will be very envious of this because it reminds him of his lack of building relationships, and he wants you all to himself. And he will not stop until that happens; until you are as depleted and void of relationships as he.

For us, the independent women, he will hit us out of the blue. This man is the author of "Flipping the Fucking Script." You will be like, WTF! He will enjoy your reaction, which is what he intended from the beginning. He will let off a barrage of dislikes and faults that you have. He will try to take you down with his observations, and many of them will not make sense to you because possibly no other man has ever pointed these "new faults" out to you. He will take everything you do as an affront to him. As an independent woman, he will perceive you as having too much masculine energy. Because he looks at women as an extension of himself, you having an opinion other than his will be received as being argumentative and hostile. Everything you say to this man will be dissected and later used against you. Most likely, this man will beat you at "dumping" before you can dump him because you may possibly still be in shock. Unlike the DB, the NGAM will never call you back, text you, and may even block your number. As mentioned, this man cuts people off like a dropped call on your damn cell phone network.

The NGAM is the reason why we must take our time with men as women. This man poses the most threats to us across the board. Out of all types of men, this man is the most likely to hit you physically. This is due to the severe control issues he has and his lack of emotions. This man holds everything in and can explode at any given time. He is also very angry, and although he may appear to have it all together from the outside, this man's ego is very fragile. He is insecure and has a very low self-esteem. The NGAM quite possibly may live a double life. Because he has such a secretive nature, he may have sexual practices that he keeps hidden. He may even be a down-low man. But no one would ever know this because he is discreet, and he will take this to the grave with him. He may even be homophobic and speak very loudly against homosexuality. The NGAM may have some sexual difficulties when dealing with you as a woman. Issues like keeping an erection and/or having unrealistic demands of you, like hours upon hours of sex with him. He lives in his head so much that his intimacy levels will be void. He just will not be able to go there emotionally like that with you. He may also have sleeping disorders or doesn't sleep very well or often. Don't be surprised by fetishes with feet and shoes. He can likely be part of the SMS scene as well as into pornography and prostitution, but only the high-class ones, though, because of his OCD issues. As an independent woman, you may experience some of this on a limited basis because, again, you will not be with him long, but a passive woman will bear the brunt of all of this. He will also engage in demeaning things with a woman sexually to degrade her.

The No-Good Ass Man, unlike the Douche Bag, will likely not change. He believes the lies he tells himself and the others. His arrogance and narcissism will not allow him to see any faults of his own or corrections he needs to make within himself, and he just never lets anyone get emotionally close enough to him to become a source of accountability. Even the low self-esteem woman who stays with him long term does not know him well. She is but a guest in his world and has very little power to impact him in any real manner, which is why he is with her. It will take professional help to possibly break through with this man for him to have a chance at any real emotional connection with another human being, but again, his ego will not allow him to reach out for that kind of help.

The good news about the No-Good Ass Man is that there are not many of them in the general population. Not nearly as many as the average good guy, the Walking Wounded or the Douche Bag for that matter.

Okay, here is a list of Characteristics to look for when encountering a No-Good Ass Man:

1. Intelligent
2. Driven in his career path
3. Manipulative
4. Controlling
5. Lack a sense of humor (dry sense of humor)
6. Showers you with gifts and attention (early on)
7. Calculating (always seems to be thinking and in his head)
8. Lacks spontaneity
9. May be wealthy monetarily
10. Doesn't have many friends (comes off as a homebody but may have a separate lifestyle that he's quite active in, that you may never know about but have moments of absences… pay attention to this ladies!!!)
11. Standoffish and Reserved
12. Materialistic
13. Has cut off relationships with family and his children, if he even has any children.
14. Womanizer (Discreet; again, you may never know this as he is not sloppy)
15. He is jealous-hearted, especially of you
16. Will label women as aggressive or hostile if they are independent-minded
17. Strange sexual practices (different from yours)
18. Will be charming (in the beginning)

19. Secretive and (Private) His phone will have more security codes on it than the pentagon
20. Anger Outbursts (Will call you out your name)
21. Flips the Script on you (Dr. Jekyle and Mr. Hide type personality)
22. Will appear to be your Champion man (in the beginning)
23. This man is dangerous for you and seeks out a way to harm you

Now, Please write down some of your definitions of what you believe a No-Good Ass man is to you that may be different than mine above.

_____
_____
_____
_____
_____
_____
_____
_____
_____
_____
_____
_____
_____
_____
_____
_____
_____
_____
_____

List some character traits you have experienced from a man you believed to be a NGAM man.

1._____

2._____

3._____

4._____

5._____

Ladies, I do not mean to make you all into these paranoid, mistrustful, and on-guard women like I have become, but we honestly must be for our own protection. There is a way to go about this, though. We do not have to be mean, hostile, or always ready for a fight. But we must set parameters for ourselves. Define what we are looking for and what we want from a man. We must come to an understanding of what we are working with these days when it comes to our man selection. Do our research, ask questions, and be watchful of what's going on around us, with the man we are giving our time to, and to whom we may be exposing our children. We also need to be realistic about our expectations of men.

Know who and what a good man is and looks like. We can stop this sense of desperation and anxiety that goes on inside us with being alone and without a man. We need to start asking those realistic questions ourselves: if our lives are being enriched by the man whom we are sharing our lives with, are we happy or miserable? Honor, loyalty, and integrity are dying attributes these days, and so when you find it in "just an average, everyday guy," you quite possibly want to hold on to that man. But not out of desperation but because you want that man in your life, and he brings something valuable to your life. People will lie to your face and not think anything about it, which is more the reason we must take our time with men, period. We must be on the defensive in a sense and play smart. We deserve better and have too much to lose to continue to be cavalier about our approach.

I think once we have done work on ourselves as women, learn to raise the bar for ourselves, and define for ourselves, we can then better pick a man who will be good for us and our families. We will stop responding to that man from a place of fear that he will leave us, and we will be better equipped should he decide to do just that.

Chapter Seven:
The Reluctant Feminist: I'm Too Lazy To Take Sides

Really, I am just too lazy. I just do not want to make the time to research what line of feminism I align myself with, who's agenda I'm supporting this year, the liberal feminist, the conservative feminist, and is there such a thing as an independent feminist? Maybe that would be the one I most identify with. I honestly just don't give a shit about taking sides. I can appreciate most of what anyone would do for the advancement of women. Hell, I can even appreciate a male feminist if there was such a thing. Is there? Anywho, all I know is that I am a woman, and there are interests that I must protect for myself and other women. We do not have to subscribe to a philosophy in order to champion women's issues. We just have to understand the basics of what benefits the woman within her culture. Yes, it does take a certain amount of organizing to accomplish these goals, which is where my respect for feminism comes into play. As women, we had to organize to make any real moves and changes; I get that. But even with that said, at the time of women's suffrage, there was not an inclusivity of all women, and that movement mainly pertained to white/Caucasian women at that time. Women and movements haven't been so inclusive of what certain demographics of women face in this culture, whether it is black/African women, Asian women, and/or Hispanic/Latin women in this country. Even as the feminist movement progressed through history and time, it was always centered on issues that pertained to white/Caucasian women. It took the civil rights movement of the 50s and 60s to blanket and cover rights for all women as a minority. Dang it, I honestly didn't mean to get that researchy there, but anywho.

I do believe feminism set a tone for women that was not well thought out and just mimicked male dominance and what is conducive to male dominance. In American culture, it is still beneficial for women to be in a committed relationship with men. When dealing with dominance of any kind in the masses, we need to understand the social constructs will always play out and in benefit to the dominance and often becomes a well-oiled machine over time. It becomes systemic and ingrained into the culture.

I cringe a bit at the word feminist. It's not that I don't value and appreciate what the feminist movement did for women and the positive impacts it did and does continue to have. But with this said, I also must recognize the negatives this movement implemented for women as well. There's always the good, the bad, and the ugly with most things. In my opinion, we just got some very bad advice and rhetoric about maneuvering in this male-dominant society in which we live. I am mostly speaking about the American culture and society as it is the only one I have lived in. We just were not taught how to play smart, and we are witnessing and experiencing the residual effects of this bad advice today in the form of high divorce rates (there is a very small number of women who do not want to be in a long-term, committed, loving relationship with one man, so please stop telling us otherwise), unwanted pregnancies, single motherhood, STDs on the rise, and poor women becoming poorer.

We were told women can do anything a man can do and should. Well, in a perfect world, this concept is true and correct. But we are not in a perfect world, and there is no area in which we have seen the worst of this advice other than sex and women. We were erroneously encouraged to have sex like a man. If they can do it, then by golly, we can! The sexual revolution was not a supportive movement for women. This was a masculine movement and a response to a masculine society. We were told we should and could wield our vaginas just like a man swings his wee wee. Well, from my previous chapters, we already know our vaginas are gold, and would you flush gold down the toilet? Give your gold away to just anyone? We were told we should be open and loose about our vaginas, literally! Well, as we all know, who wants a loose vagina, literally? Nothing should be loosey-goosey about the vajayjay. I agree; as women, we should be able to do what we want with our vaginas. But giving it away to every Tom's hairy dick is not a good move. It's a very bad play, ladies, when we are dealing with the construct of male dominancy. It is also no coincidence that much of this attitudinal change for women to become loosey with their vaginas also coincided with the onset of the acceptance and use of birth control and soon followed by way of DNA/Paternity testing, which in turn ushered in the Child Support BUSINESS. Remember, folks, this is a well-oiled machine. Social constructs are put into play, and we then respond to them. I am not going to get too much into my social conspiracy theories at this time; I will save those for another book.

In essence, the Sexual Revolution minimized our power and the control of our vaginas. We basically handed over our vaginas to men and the male-dominated system we operate in. Therefore, we see today such a flamboyant response to female beauty and sexuality. These are not feminine-based definitions but male-centered definitions. We are just along for the ride, literally and figuratively. And most women are quite annoyed and irritated by these definitions and imagery of who and what a woman is. We feel helpless to change it; therefore, many just go along with it or try to emulate what is put out there for us. From how we are supposed to dress to be pretty, what we are supposed to weigh to be attractive, and what our vaginas are even supposed to look like!

As independent women, we must think critically about what we really want and what works in our lives. We were also told within the feminist movement that we can outdo men and do not need men. I agree we do not need men to survive as long as we are already born to this world and can live in it without a man. But do I need a man if I am in a relationship with a man and to feel like I am thriving in that relationship? Yes, I do! I need him to do his part and to add to my life as I would hope I would to his. But it is not about outdoing men. And I do believe many feminist agendas have since recanted some of this rhetoric. But I am not completely sure as, again, I am too lazy to do much research on the matter.

Now, we have an abundance of books that are masculine-centered, directing us to think like a man. Are we really buying into this shit? A bit of news, ladies: no matter how hard you try, you will not be able to think like a man. We do not have to think like men to understand a male dominant society and culture. Certain privileges come with being a male in this culture, just like there are certain privileges that come with being a white/Caucasian person in this country. I do not have to be white to understand this or think like a white person, whatever that means. I could never think like a white person because I do not have the life experience of what it is to be white/Caucasian in America. But if I think critically, I can understand how our society responds to white privilege and why racism and prejudice are still very much alive in our country. The same goes for understanding male privilege.

I can understand male privilege from a feminine perspective. I think it is very important for us to stay centered with our feminine perspective. In order to do this, we must first understand what femininity is and what drives it. Yes, some of it is environmental and the things we are taught, and some of it is physiological and spiritual, in my opinion. As women, we need to understand what is in our best interest and for other women. What is advancing us, and what is holding us back? These will be things on a personal individual level as well as a macro and worldly common level.

What we need to be doing as women is thinking critically with our feminine minds like a woman should. We need to protect our interests that may have very little to do with men and their definitions. However, we need to know their definitions and understand them; we do not have to conform to them. Once we start to operate from our own definitions and parameters, we can begin to understand their reactions and responses to us a bit more clearly. Becoming or being an independent woman will always appear as a type of masculine energy in a male-dominated society. Even if a woman is quite feminine in her dress, her walk, her hair, and her mannerism, if that woman is running her own company, making decisions without the approval of the man, then eight times out of ten, she is termed as bitchy, manly, and quite possibly aggressive. American culture often places women in the sidekick role: the nurse, the aide, the assistant, and rarely, the owner. Now, of course, we see the images on TV, which, if left up to that medium, we would continue to remain in the dark about the realities of women and independence forever. Again, who runs Hollywood? The reality is that women are still viewed as an extension of men. Not equals, as I have stated throughout this book. Talk to the female actresses in that industry about their pay rate and roles as compared to men, and I'm sure some will be willing to give you the skinny on that topic.

You may say my traditionalist views expressed earlier are contrary to what I am stating in this chapter. And, I would say not at all. Again, it's not about us outdoing men or competing with men we are in relationships with. That is the difference: being in a relationship as opposed to being within our careers and work environments. We are still our own persons as women. Men have their roles, and as women, we have ours when it comes to our personal relationships. Neither is above the other or below. We are equals. Just because we don't do the exact same jobs within the parameters of a relationship (Traditional views vs Non-Traditional views) doesn't mean we don't play for the same team or are not contributing just as much as the other gender. It's more so about us accepting or even wanting more defined positions within that relationship and/or even relating to duties within the relationship. An agreement of sorts. Last time I checked, I could do anything a man could, but do I want to do all things a man can do within the parameters of my relationship with my man? Not at all. Do I need a man to do certain things for me? Not at all. Do I want my man to do certain things for me? I sure do. That's what it comes down to for me. Now, in our work environments, we most definitely need to present a healthy amount of competition towards any gender if we are to see advancement and promotion. I think, as women, we can confuse the two, and men even have complaints on this front that a woman wants to be the boss at work and then come home and boss him around. There must be a certain amount of finesse when dealing with authority in our work life and then with our men. This is something I am still learning. As we have also learned in this book, the male ego must be stroked at certain times if that man is to feel respected and loved by any woman, whether independent or not. But as independent women, we can be a bit heavy-handed when it comes to our authority. This is where remembering our femininity and our nurturing spirits can aid us. We should not have resentments about turning on a softer touch when it comes to our men. Yes, some men are just pansy asses, but if you are with that pansy ass man, then you need to figure out what strokes his ego and not if you are to remain in a relationship with that man and keeping the peace is important to you.

Most people would label me a feminist, and although I'm not a fan of labels, I don't care so much. People label people all the time; it's just what we do. I will not subscribe to those labels and allow people to put me into a box. If I had to label myself or align myself with a movement, it would be the Womanist movement, which is steadily growing in popularity. This movement appears to embody a collaborative effort with men as opposed to a competitive one that the feminist movement fosters. The womanist approach zones in on cultivating our feminine needs and interests through a woman's perspective rather than a watered-down version of masculine needs, as the feminist agenda seems to always piggyback from what men's needs are, making us copycats rather than authentic and separate beings. I have stated, and hopefully have shared throughout this book, that I am a multifaceted woman and person, as most people are and should be allowed to be.

I am coming more into an understanding that MANeuvering intelligently in a man's world requires a skill set in understanding the male ego. American culture bolsters the male ego and inflates it, basically because men run shit in this country. This is not to say women don't have power; we have more than we know and more than what we are tapping into, which is the whole point of this chapter, hell, possibly this entire book.

Feminism and independence have always been synonymous. But even today, an independent woman is spoken about in negative terms, especially by insecure men who just do not get that they really do want an independent woman and will be most productive with an independent woman. Men must understand they do not want a woman who 'needs' them. And we are even hearing men state they do not want a "needy" woman, that other "N" word, but so many still gravitate towards women who are just that. I have argued rounds with men, especially about independent women, stating they do not 'need' men. And trust me, it is said with contempt. Again, even on this topic, men oscillate back and forth because they themselves just do not know what they want. People voice things and say things all the time, but their thought processing and actions do something else entirely. I do not want another human being needing me for anything that is outside of a child who needs me as a parent to grow and thrive. Even after that child becomes an adult, that adult child should no longer need their parents to survive, and if they do, then your parenting skills were lacking, js. This goes for a significant other as well. We should not be parenting significant others.

An independent woman can often be a lonely position if you do not have other independent women in your immediate circle. Not only do some men respond to you negatively, but other women can respond to you negatively as well. Most of us are type A personalities, Alpha female personalities. I know this about myself, and I do try to tone it down and be more collaborative. However, we are decision-makers by nature, and who has time to wait for people to make up their f'ing minds, right? Only men are supposed to think this way. It's not very ladylike to be so assertive. We are typically labeled as overbearing and sometimes not team players, and please do not try to micromanage us; we will come out with fangs and claws. We make great supervisors, CEOs, managers, and administrators if we understand our nature and we have tapped into our flexibility, along with understanding the necessity of maintaining our femininity. But an Independent woman who does not have a grasp of her nature, there is no worse tyrant. I have been under independent women who have taken on that persona of outdoing men at everything, who have lost their sense of femininity and the glorious qualities that being a strong, independent feminine woman can bring to any environment. Again, healthy competition and drive are a must as women if we are to have success, but channeling immature male characteristics is not the way to go at all as a woman, and when I was under that type of authority, it was not a fun situation and quite often women like this can inspire mutiny aboard ship. Just the same as a man can in this same position, but I think with women, it's even less tolerated. No one respects a tyrant. But I do think that there can be a negative backlash against a strong, independent woman regardless of whether she is a tyrant or not. But if that woman is fair, she will foster respect from both men and women alike. They may not like her, but they will respect her.

There is no need to be a snob, mean and hateful as an independent woman, and this is simply just an immature woman, which I will explain in another chapter. That's not what independence is. If you must exert yourself along those lines, then you are missing the point. It's okay to be assertive, blunt, to the point, concise, decisive, and passionate… but in all those things, be fair and decent. Treat people fairly, with integrity and respect. As an independent woman, this is what will take us further. We do not have to go around wiping folks' noses and being the office cheerleader; lord knows I don't have much patience to assure others and their moods. But with this said, we can still be sensitive to others, their feelings and what they may be going through in their lives. Although the independent woman doesn't care too much about brownies or cool points from others, or maybe it just doesn't affect us so much, we still need to be mindful of setting the tone in which we can be received more readily. Again, it comes down to respect, and when you are fair, even during tough decisions, you will still garner respect. Many of us have to grow into this understanding about who we really are. I'm still learning, and I'm open to knowing more and fine-tuning this independent cast I am molded within. I have come to accept it, but I still need more answers as to who she is and the "ever-evolving" of *Her.*

Chapter Eight:
Who Is The Independent Woman? Not Completely Sure, But She Demands To Find Out…

As I continue my journey of self-discovery and understanding who and what an independent woman really is. I have concluded that I do not know if there are any definitive definitions of this woman. I would imagine the independent woman would have to be a woman who is evolving and growing, hence even the title of independence.

In this chapter, I will make some attempts at defining who the independent woman is or who I think I am as a self-proclaimed independent woman. Most of what I share in this chapter is just common-sense guesses, opinions, and my truths at this moment in time. One thing I know for sure is that society and American culture have vilified the independent woman. You said the "I" word and then got fingers pointed at you for even associating yourself with such a thing. The independent woman has been vilified so much that even some women want nothing to do with the term or title, even if they quite possibly are the epitome of what an independent woman is. Additionally, many men equate the term independent woman with the title witch and bitch on a regular basis, and they can be quite suspicious of us and the male bashing hate we spew. *eye roll.

Before I make my attempts at defining who the independent woman is, let me first reveal who the independent woman is not and dispel some myths about us that I do believe are quite unfair.

Independent women are not men haters. Quite the contrary, we love MEN. What we are fed up with is men being allowed to behave badly and get away with it. To the point, even decent, good men are starting to get affected by this, making it that much more difficult for women even to recognize a good man anymore.

Independent women do not bash MEN, but we do bash males who claim to be men. I like how the relationship coach Tony Gaskins Jr terms these males "Grown Boys". Grown boys are males who are emotionally immature but in grown men's bodies. They act and respond in an emotionally cripple manner by engaging in immature things from preying on women and their emotions, cheating, lying to get their needs met, using, and discarding other human beings without much thought, and are moral derelicts, to say the least. These are the men we bash and want to get the hint that we want them exterminated from the general population.

Another myth about the independent woman is that we do not "need" men. I touched on this a little earlier. This "need" thing should be clarified a little. People typically make this reference without any clear indication as to what 'need' they are referring to.

Firstly, no grown adult able-bodied person should "need" another adult person to survive in this world and often, when this need is referenced, it is as if the other person cannot live without the significant other. That it is a survival need, and is dangerous to even think you need another person to survive, that you cannot go on living without them. What people should be referencing here are relationship needs, not survival needs. Most people confuse the two or use them interchangeably or do not think about it at all within the realms of a romantic relationship.

Independent *women* do not need men to survive or this is called co-dependency at best. When you need people this way, it is when you see them follow each other into hell and back and even take children with them. We will use the case of the abused/battered woman who believes in her mind she cannot live without that male who is abusing her, and quite possibly, abusing her children as well. There is a lot of psychosis in needing people along these survival lines, and I think most independent women understand this and just will not go there with a man especially.

Now, the type of need the independent woman does subscribe to are relationship needs. I do need a man to do his part in the relationship if I am to grow and thrive in it. If I'm going to grow in that relationship, I need that man to meet me halfway and do the necessary things that will help me feel loved, secure and wanted in the relationship. Relationship needs are key to a productive relationship, and we should even use the "need" word often when referring to them. Relationships are mutual. If one is not doing their part, then the relationship falls apart. Or if one is doing more than the other to sustain the relationship, then that one gets overworked and burned out, and then they just stop working as well. So, relationship needs must be at the forefront of building a strong foundation, not survival needs. I really do not want another adult looking to me to save their life. Besides our own children who do depend on us to survive (we must feed them, clothe them, shelter them, etc.), we should never look to another adult to care for us in this manner or have to in order to sustain a relationship with them. Otherwise, they rely on us so emotionally that they cannot function without us around. Most people mistake these codependent tendencies as a strong love when nothing could be further from the truth.

Another myth is that we are "Strong". Again, yes, we are emotionally strong, but even the strongest person wants someone in their corner cheering them on. Emotionally, we can handle ourselves in ways that are productive for our lives, but believe me, we want a helper. Most independent women want to rely on a man emotionally. We want an emotionally safe place with our men. We want to discard that layer of strength at times. I think this is probably an independent woman's true quest with a man. But what we often encounter is some men cannot handle that strength and, as previous chapters have detailed, react negatively to it as opposition rather than independence. Some men need to understand that we do have a mind of our own, can make decisions, and hopefully, with their help and sometimes without it. Again, that's what being an individual person is about: making decisions for our lives and living within that life's framework. To be fair, many independent women do struggle with loosening that hold and releasing some of that superwoman persona. This persona often comes from a place of fear and mistrust because of past issues and relationships that just weren't reliable in allowing the loosening of the reins. But if a male comes along who is patient with that woman and who is that reliable man she wants and whom she can consistently depend on to do as he says he will do, that woman will loosen her hold of control and welcome that help.

Now that we have the myths out of the way let's move forward in defining the independent woman. Again, I do not think there is a clear definition of the independent woman and because our independence is constantly changing, so will definitions or the things that independent women may subscribe to.

I think an independent woman understands her independence has very little to do with men at all. The independent woman recognizes herself as a separate soul in this world. She is not an extension of the man but can be an addition to the man to equal something.

Secondly, the independent woman is a free-thinking woman who has paved her path by the decisions she has made that quite possibly have had little male influence, and she may have been by herself outside of a relationship with a male most of the way. This could have been by her choice or circumstances. Through circumstances, many independent women may have found themselves in a state of single parenthood, where we have most likely raised our children predominantly by ourselves. Again, this is a circumstance she may have just found herself in and likely not wanted. Many independent women understand and value the father's role in their children's lives. One thing that being an independent woman does is it enhances an appreciation level for men and men who do their part, whether in a relationship with them or caring for their children outside of a relationship. I think most independent women will work with the father more readily than any other woman, i.e., the needy woman. A needy woman often needs validation in many areas and can be unreasonably emotional to her children's detriment. An independent woman is not going to hold on to a man whom she is no longer in a relationship with because she knows and understands she is not bound to that man in some unrealistic manner only because they were together once. We take our time for ourselves and may even cry and moan a bit, but only a bit. There is no other woman who moves on (emotionally) faster from a failed relationship than the independent woman. We have too many things going on in our lives to stay stuck on a man for too long. For one, our children are our biggest motivators to get it together, and if we have help from their fathers, great, but if not, we do what we must to ensure our children are cared for. We are not looking to play games with the father about seeing his children or withhold visits to punish the father for leaving us. But because we are independent, we know our children will be cared for regardless of whether the father is doing his part or not, and so, him visiting his children is okay with us. In fact, I and many other independent women have been known to go out of our way to ensure those visits with the father.

When it comes to defining the independent woman, one cannot discuss this woman without discussing the intimidation factor that is ever present. This aspect of being an independent woman probably affects me the most in regard to the fact that I do not want to be intimidating to anyone. And often, I'm surprised that others believe me to be intimidating at all. Men have often made this 'accusation' to me on more than one occasion. Again, a woman being sure-footed and confident is often talked about and sounds good on paper in American culture, but for women who are this way, society bucks up against them, and not just men, women too, will take issue with the independent woman. Another independent woman will not be intimidated with most other independent women because they just get it; they, too, are sure of themselves. It is typically insecure and immature women with power, quite possibly positional power, that take us as an affront to them, as questioning their authority. This is how you can tell the difference between a true independent woman and an immature woman who has gained some power within maybe the confines of her work/employment. This type of woman will display several insecurities. The insecure woman will always see questions as a form of questioning her authority, especially by other women. The independent woman knows that questioning is how we get ahead in this world. Collaborating with others is how we gain access to growth within our workplace. Independent women fare better in environments of diversity and the least in female-driven work environments. If you have been paying attention to this chapter, you should be able to deduce why this is the case.

From the description above, one would get the impression that the independent woman is always an 'outspoken' Alpha female type. This could not be further from the truth either. I am an Alpha female if I have to be and can tap into her at any time. But I am most comfortable being in the background, reserved a bit at times, as I just do not have to be the center of attention. Or feel like I am in command and top dog. I am neither loud nor boisterous unless I am drinking with friends and/or just want to be. I think many independent women just do not feel such burdens of having to conform to the mood of others, and we can be flexible and go with things more. Again, our personalities can range widely, but we are not attention whores for the reason of our independence. Being an attention whore is contrary to independence.

In defining this woman, I do believe the true independent woman is not lacking in self-esteem where she must get feeding from outside influences to act in certain ways to appease others. A people pleaser is not an independent woman, although she can be nice and friendly. Not being people pleasers may, at times, come off as us being a bit dismissive or not caring as much as we "should." We care and love deeply just like anyone else, and it's just that we do not necessarily feel the proclivity as other women to dote and wait on others. We can be service-driven with a heart of gold, but it's strictly by our terms and because we want to do it. You may even hear true independent women say things like, "My children are not my life." Some women or people, in general, may hear this and wonder if we are nurturing if we feel this way. Independent women most likely raise very independent children from themselves as we just do not want our children up under us, nor do we feel a need to smother them with our mothering. We also have quite loving and affectionate relationships with our children, and we really do not care what others think about this with our parenting either. We do not look for affirmation from others very often, as already indicated, which again, as mentioned in previous chapters, can come off as a type of masculine energy to people, men and women, who do not understand it. Or, again, we can be labeled as intimidating. Many independent women also may not have any children at all. They have just decided that children do not fit into the equation of their lives. These women are especially vilified because how dare they decide about their own bodies and motherhood. Motherhood in itself says, "My choice to do as I please with my body and my life." Often, women who choose not to have children are also looked upon as not nurturing, and that is just not true as well.

Most independent women are also quite smart, intelligent and with common sense. I call this the Intelligence Factor.

This could be a large portion of the reason why so many of us are single, and we believe this to be much of the case. One thing independent women do understand is that many males, on average, do not want a smart woman. Now men will argue us down and talk out of both sides of their necks on this one, and all the while, he's shacked up with Susie Q Dumbass; remember her from down the street? Smart women can use deductive and inductive reasoning like nobody's business, and if we can use that kind of reasoning, most likely, we can see through guys trying to push a lot of bullshit onto us. So, many guys (those males) just will not even go there with us and waste their time. Yaaay!!

It seems that the smarter and more independent women become, the higher the divorce rates go up. As a black woman, I must mention here that the divorce rates and not marrying at all amongst blacks are at epidemic levels. There is also a direct relation to college-educated black women who are outnumbering black men in record numbers, in raw numbers and degrees. Oh, and white women, don't you get too comfortable here, as your divorce rates/marrying rates are not too much ahead of ours, and it will be pretty leveled off within just a few short years. So, this should raise a few eyebrows when it comes to the topic of men really wanting an intelligent and smart woman, and most of us will not dumb ourselves down to be with and "keep" a man. Believe me, I have tried. It lasted like half a conversation, and he was on to the fact that I was "actually smart"… and in those very words. Dammit! I didn't see him again. Yay, I guess.

As human beings, we like having our way and to MANipulate. A male who can manipulate a woman to go along with him and his shenanigans will choose the dumber woman. There are still quite a few women out there who want a man so desperately that they allow that man to manipulate them and will stay with that male or accept his misbehaving for quite a long time to keep him. Independent women just do not last that long with selfish men who only want their way. Either we are out, or they are. Selfish men run from us. It's a good thing, but it is still quite sad that so many men are choosing to stay emotionally crippled instead of raising their standards to work with an emotionally sound woman. It is not unusual for some of the most broken women to always have an available male to choose from. But make no mistake, ladies, these are not the males you want to be around you and your children. These men are users and abusers and will leave you high and dry or with a wet ass, as that is the reason many of them are there. To prove my point, how many men have "you" gone through in the last 2 years or so? If it is more than 4-5 men, then ladies, your vagina is a revolving door for these types of males, and you need to close the shop and get some knowledge as to what is going on with you.

Being an intelligent woman also translates into higher salaries than a man, and this topic is still taboo in American culture. This is the Money Factor. We still, on average, make less when it comes to the dollar itself, but we quite possibly have more dollars than some of these men in the dating pool. As mentioned in a previous chapter, independent women hold jobs well, have been in their career fields for several years and make great supervisors and administrators. Many of us also have businesses or multiple side hustles with several streams of income. Some men still need to come into the new millennium on this issue. Many still find it emasculating for a woman to make more money. What can be emasculating about your woman buying you a new toy, like a car... but okay. As women, we find nothing emasculating about getting gifts from our men and even expect it at times. (Okay, that was a bit cheeky, lol.). I don't mind buying my guy things and paying for things, but in turn, even as the independent woman that I am, I want my guy to take care of me and make me feel special with gifts, adoration, affection, and attention as well. As independent women, we think about our money much the same as men. This is something I have come to terms with for myself. Also mentioned in a previous chapter, I will never merge ALL my finances with a man. In this day and age, it is just not a wise thing to do, ladies!! Now, if you want to hold on to the Barbie dream house fantasy, then count this as "you have been warned." This does bring about the discussion of the legal merging of finances once a woman marries a man. Ladies, if you have acquired your money on your own, you need to sign a prenup! Point… Blank… Period! Enough said on that, or remain unmarried and still maintain a committed relationship with that man. As I have aged, I have concluded about legal marriages that the government may benefit more from them than we do. But that is another book or article, at least.

In conclusion, the independent woman can be many things to different people. We are evolving as time passes because we must; that is what being an independent woman is all about. We cannot stay stuck and hold on to unrealistic fantasies about relationships, men, and the world around us. We view ourselves as separate souls from our men and willing to forge our own way in this world. And I want to emphasize that this doesn't mean we do not want a man next to us or helping us. It's just that we do not need that man to survive or to pave that path necessarily with us, and certainly not for us. We recognize our independence as our human right. Men are never questioned on their independence, and they just are. Well, we want that same courtesy, and we do not have to have anyone's permission to demand it.

Chapter Nine:
The Cougar, The Cub Scout, Interracial Dating, Misogynistic Violence, Lesbians And Other Controversial Things…Where Is All Of This Going?

I try not to subscribe to any philosophy of any kind in a religious dogmatic manner, but I do read, write notes, follow up on trends, go to scholarly lectures, Google stuff, cross reference contradictions, read abstract studies and have a mind of my own to come to certain conclusions as any of us should. I do have a degree in psychology if that helps you to receive the things I'm about to say. I have worked in the human and social service field for close to 30 years now if you need that information as well. Personally, I do not think anyone needs any credentials to know and understand human behavior and history. In fact, our ancestors relied on their own wisdom, discussions and counsel with others, and spiritual intuition of their own to make their conclusions and decisions on life. Somehow, these folks with letters at the end of their names, who have attended fancy schools, seemed to have hijacked the open forum to think and apply our own understanding. These people who think they have a monopoly on thinking and information have done more damage to us than anyone, but I digress. When it's all said, you just need to know a few people, have lived a few years into adulthood, read and pay attention. You can come to as many conclusions as the folks who put on the elaborate tests, stats compiling and all that. Yes, I appreciate people who do labor in the field of research and share all that information with us; it can be very informational and educational, but often by the end of that study, you're like, wow, I could have saved them a lot of damn money and told them that shit!! Yes, I understand there are scholarly people here who have formed words and have assigned data and research to much of what I talk about in this book, whether good, bad, or indifferent; I have even gone to some of their lectures. But I just refuse to lay all that rhetoric onto people. I am a lay person who just needs things said to me in plain old English, and I want to understand what people are saying without all the fluffery of big words... so please do not use old English perse.

Human behavior is quite predictable (yet complex.) History has ways of repeating itself in different packages as well.

What does this chapter have to do with the single independent woman? Glad you asked! Well, in this chapter, I hope to detail some of what I think is happening for independent women, how we are evolving or devolving, for that matter, and what is on the horizon for women in American culture particularly. I will be cheeky at times, humorous as well as passionate. So, take it as you may, I really do not care, remember? But I do believe the rise of the independent woman is shaping and reshaping our culture daily. I believe we will encounter some great things as a result but also some possibly gruesome things as well. I am not a mind reader, nor do I know the future, but again, if we are paying attention, understand an inkling of human behavior and can refer to history, many things can be revealed to us in advance and be great indicators of what's to come.

One particular occurrence on the rise for independent women that we see more, even now, is the relations between the Cougar and the Cub. That is the older woman and the younger man. Now, again, referring to HIStory, this is nothing new. It's only new for women, or more accepted and publically so. Men have been engaging in philandering with younger women since the beginning of time. But what is changing is the dispersing of power and access to that power by women. Any time anyone carries a certain amount of power and wants to be in a relationship with another human being, that other being must be willing to accept the positional power the other has. As women and men start to level off in the power arena that they carry, there is bound to be some bumping of heads, if you will. As I have already detailed in other chapters, some men struggle to accept a woman who makes more money than them or who is more powerful than they are. Not only are the men just not wasting their time going there with "those women," but neither are those women with older men of their age group. We are not quite at the level men are with this attitude change as they have mastered taking advantage of younger people. Okay, here's my slip on how I really feel about this issue. But I will still speak on it because I do believe it's quite relevant to us as independent women and the positions we are finding ourselves in.

We see examples of this especially when we look to celebrities, the Madonnas, Demi Moore, JLo's of the world and in those industries that are helping to create very powerful women. As more industries open to women and women create a space for us in these industries to advance our wealth, we will continue to see women with younger men. I'm sure these women are with these younger men for various reasons. I am almost certain that, if asked, many will detail their power and status and how it may be just easier with a younger man with less power and status. Again, men have been doing this for centuries. They had it a bit easier and had more access, primarily due to our history of women's oppression in this country and on the global stage. Again, this is just human behavior playing out and people responding to the social cues as the world shapes and forms with us. We can choose to respond blindly, or we can be informed as we move with the changes and make our own decisions as to how we will respond. I know for me personally, there is nothing a younger man can do for me, but then, I'm not a financially powerful woman. Yet! And if any of those cougars come pawing after my 30-year-old son, they will have mama bear to contend with.

As men find themselves in positions of competition in the workforce, marketplace, and business with women, which is already the case, more men will consent to the idea of women in positions above and greater than them. This will also translate into the romantic forum as well. Some men are even verbalizing they prefer women who make more money presently. Now, I do report that they "say" this, but again, this is a work in progress. Quite often, people say things they don't really believe or only do halfheartedly. It is certainly PC for men to say they want an intelligent, powerful, and wealthy woman. Who wants to admit they are a male chauvinist and prefer women they can manipulate? But some men really are trying to be more progressive about this. Men also have their learning curves with these changes. They do not understand us and our evolution any more than we do. They just have the advantage of having things play in their favor more because of the male privilege. Men are responding to the same cues we are, but again, with that advantage going with being a male in American culture. As the independent woman pushes the envelope and continues to trailblaze, men will not have a choice but to give in. Some will be more willing to take advantage of it than to fight against it, i.e., in the case of the cub, the younger man. A younger man with an older woman has a different exchange of benefits than that of the younger woman and older man. If an older man has secured a younger and physically appealing woman, you best believe he is paying dearly for that woman financially. Women are attracted to security. That older man will have to be offering that younger woman security in the things she wants for her to stay. But for the younger man and older woman, he is not there so much for the money. Although she can provide him with some financial gains, that younger man is there more for his freedom. Freedom? Yes, his freedom. Most younger men understand that another younger woman who is on the same level as him wants him to commit to her and be in that traditional relationship. Well, as (also) indicated earlier in previous chapters, there is just not much incentive these days for men, especially younger men, to even want to be and stay in a "constricted" monogamous relationship. An older and independent woman who doesn't "need" that man for the purpose of committing will be and become more appealing to the younger man. Therefore, he can maintain his freedom more readily with an older, more settled woman. Don't get mad at me; I do not make the rules. Human behavior 101 and social norms, societal cues 101. Just look around you. As women become more established in wealth and power, we will begin to see more of these relationships developing. For me personally, again, I do not have a desire for a younger man. That could change as things change in my life. Who knows!

Another happening and a change that's coming is in the area of interracial dating and marrying. As again mentioned in previous chapters, internet dating has opened access to so many different people that I believe this will change the racial fabric of our world; where we will begin to see this trend, more will be amongst black women. Also mentioned, there's no secret that black women out-degree and out-educate their black male counterparts, and doing so in record numbers. Also, again, we have already discussed the relations of women and education and intelligence with higher rates of being single. A high number of black women are single, and yes, I know what the statistic says, but again, I will let you go look that up for yourself. Now, don't start with those bogus reports about black women being unmarriageable due to some attitudinal problem or because we are not pretty enough. The things we will still believe in astound me. Reports like that are pushing agendas of some kind, and beware of things that just do not make any sense. Again, think critically, ladies.

What does make sense about this is that black women outnumber black men, some believe as high as 12 to 1. So even if every black woman wanted to be with a black man, 11 would be shit out of luck. Not to mention, these numbers include black men who may not be accessible to black women, who may be incarcerated, homosexual, or just not into black women. One then begins to see the dire situation that so many black women who are college-educated and gaining power in this world are finding themselves. Author Ralph Richard Banks details this plight of the black woman beautifully in his book "Is Marriage for White People: How the African American Marriage Decline Affects Everyone." He details how if black women want to be in a long-lasting relationship with a male who is on the same intellectual and academic level, they will have to marry outside of the black man. Banks even goes on to suggest that doing so will start to mend the marriage decline in the black community. It really comes down to supply and demand and simple math. The less accessible you are, the more you are wanted, and the more desperate you are, the more misuse you will undergo. Again, do not shoot the messenger. I have my own very controversial opinions about interracial dating that you can find on social media and in my articles somewhere online.

Now, I will say collectively, for black women, money, power, and education is all new thing for us in this country. But what is not new for us is being in the workforce and laboring to get ahead. You guys may remember that slavery thing just a little over a hundred and fifty years ago. We came into this "established" country laboring. I mentioned "established" here as it relates to the Africans brought over during the Transatlantic Slave trade; there were already groups of Africans who were here before the United States was established. But that is another book. We also did not have the protection of our male counterparts and have learned the art of fighting for what we want and being very resourceful in doing so. That is what survival is. If there is one demographic female group that is labeled and sometimes unfavorably labeled as independent, it is that of the black African American woman. We are the poster children for female Independence. This has been a thorn in our sides. A benefit but also a liability at times. But as black women are finding themselves in a place of power, wealth, and authority, we are also finding ourselves outside of the inner circle with black males. And so, dating/marrying out would benefit us not only emotionally but financially as well because we have the support from a man whom we could relate to on an equal or similar level of intellect, education, and finances. That man will most likely be acquiring wealth at the same level as us. As a bit of an African Nationalist, ooops... it's out! Again, I do not subscribe to labels, but I am more in favor of black people marrying each other and building up our culture, communities, and families first. My personal belief is that the number one thing black people can do to benefit our people in this country is to marry, commit to each other, stay together, and raise our children together. This will, in turn, change the fabric of black America and us thriving in this country and in our urban black communities where gentrification is pushing many out of family homes and stifling black-owned business growth.

With the above stated, I still cannot tell black women to believe as I do with knowing what I know and tell them to live a life of solitude because of the lack of choices in black men. The reality for many black women is that black men are not waiting on us. At this point in my life, I would love to be in a relationship with a black man, and I will continue to wait for that one for me. I am single by choice because I just cannot settle on what has been presented to me by the limited candidates that I have come across. I'd like to emphasize my strong desire to see an increase in Black marriages and partnerships. However, it's crucial to acknowledge the current scarcity of such unions for Black women, primarily because of the demographic imbalance. This is a very real issue for black women, which also poses many social issues for those who want to be in relation with a black male. Unfortunately, many are single and miserable and are not quite sure why. There is just a lack of viable black men for the black independent woman who is searching for a man on the same level she has acquired. Often, these facts are mistaken as a type of black-man bashing when it is simply a reality. Black women will have to come to a decision on what they want for themselves. Do they remain single, date/marry out, or do they settle with a black man whom they may have little in common with or are not compatible? Or do they turn to polygamy and simply man share with other women? Although, I am not a particular fan of polly relationships for my life, I do believe it can be a real choice for some black women who still want to be with a black man. But please, ladies, if you go down that road, just make sure it's not on the bullshit. Those relationships can be just as dysfunctional as monogamous relationships, if not more, for the sheer number of people involved. Do your research and use common sense.

Another area for women that needs attention and concern is the topic of misogyny. We have touched on misogyny and this thirst to pound the pussy mercilessly by males in American culture a bit already; however, I believe more concentration on this desire to "beat" the pussy is definitely in order. Yes, these are song titles. We also see this desire to strong-arm the pussy into submission in Hollywood movies, porn, "art," etc.

I have always believed since I have been an adult female that women coming into power, education, and wealth incite a rebellious response from some men and, actually, a great number of men. This is the gruesome side to gaining and pushing independence as women in this country and most other countries as well. When a woman begins to exert her independence within her immediate culture truly, there will be a response. The response will reflect what the laws are in that culture and how strong they will be. When it comes to the negative responses, most often, that response has to do with misogyny, abuse, and rape. A pounding of the pussy into submission and sometimes literally. We see this play out in ungodly reports in impoverished countries and in countries where women still struggle to gain certain human rights. In American culture, we take for granted the human liberties we do have as women. I'm almost certain that other women of those impoverished countries are baffled at why we do not take advantage of those liberties more, by being more protective of who we give ourselves to and by not putting ourselves in bad situations with men who do and can abuse us. We do not have to, like those women in those impoverished countries; they do not have much of a choice. It is never a woman's fault to be raped and abused, but with that said, sometimes, we are just being dumb with the situations we put ourselves in. Again, we are just not being smart and wise. We hear the songs about pounding the pussy, we dance to them, and we buy them and support them with our money. We let men get away with calling us out of our names in the name of "fun." I think I counted in one song a woman being called a "hoe" and "bitch" 30 times by the end of the song. And we do not even get upset anymore when we are referred to as objects. Some of us want to be viewed as objects and objectify ourselves for that male attention. Those "Pick mes'."

I certainly speculate, especially in American culture, as women are gaining an understanding of the power they have in their pussies and what they do with them and/or allow others to with it, this aspect of misogyny and abuse is going to worsen. Especially as we do wizen up and start pushing against it more. Men are already quite violent towards women, and it is rarely even discussed anymore outside of the glorified media stories. We even have men complaining now with the audacity that they are being abused by women more. What the Fuck! Are you kidding me? Now, I'm not saying that women can't be just as violent as men when they are. But women are still not nearly as violent as men in numbers, and it's like men are being brainwashed to believe women are more violent towards them. Women who have a platform must speak more against violence towards women. Bring attention to this every single day. Men who have mothers, daughters, sisters, and female counterparts they care about need to speak against violence toward women and not allow other men to get away with even talking about "accepted" violence against women. Beating the pussy is a form of violence. It is a direct form of violence against a woman, her femininity, and womanhood.

As mentioned, bringing the pussy under submission is the goal, and of course, this is not witnessed any more blatantly than in the sex arena and industry. We all know what porn is. Everybody seems to know what porn is now. It used to be that pornography was a whole other world separated and hidden from the mainstream culture. Not anymore. And before I continue, let me dissipate the forming prude alert that's ringing in your ears. I am no prude. I believe in getting freaky with your man, lap dancing, and get you a damn pole if you want. Take care of your business when it comes to pleasing your partner. With that said, we do not need to see it; keep it behind closed doors.

There is no reason for your sexual escapades to be on display in mainstream culture. The only reason it is so prevalent is to push the agenda of desensitization. Desensitizing is a powerful tool of control. So, as we see more images of women being abused in a sexual manner, we just begin to accept it as something that is normal. We normalize it. Abuse and physical pain to another human being should never be normalized. Now, I'm not saying throw the baby out with the bathwater here. I like my Netflix shows, too. Some are even quite violent. None of them puts violence against women on a pedestal, though. There was a novel that gained great media attention a few years ago. I won't mention the title because I don't need to in order to make my point. But the book glorified the aspect of bringing a woman into submission with sexual aggression from a male. This young woman was immature, rather infantile and pubescent in her responses to this male. The male was holding most of the cards, and he manipulated her through control, sex, and emotional abuse. When I first tried to read the book, I couldn't even get past the first two chapters. Then I gave it another try and made it to just past the middle of the book. I threw the book away in the trash shortly after that. There was nothing I found titillating or sensual at all in that book. But what astounded me most was the female response to this book. The media packaged this book beautifully and convinced women in droves that through sexual manipulation, it is okay for a male to abuse a woman. It still baffles me that so many women fell for this and still are, as there have been several books in the series and even a movie made, I believe.

When it comes to misogyny, the force behind it is male privilege. Men benefit from the oppression of women and keeping them in their place. This is the reality of human behavior. When it comes to privilege, no one wants to admit they benefit and will argue you down about it. Who wants to give up a 30% discount? That is what privilege does, and some folks get even more of a discount depending on how many categories of privilege they may be in. We all can possibly receive discounts when it comes to cultural norms and where we are in any given situation and time, even in history. For example, we see privilege in people who are slim and trim now. They receive literal discounts on clothing, flights, and possibly job interviews to even have more access to potential partners because of what society and our norms say about people who are slim and trim. These are not things any of us want to admit, but talk to an overweight person or someone deemed obese, and they sure will tell you about the discrimination they go through daily.

Male privilege is a real thing, just like any other privilege. Some folks have the luxury of combining the privileges of being male, slim, white, etc. And so, you can begin to see the picture of privilege and what those benefits can be and are. When one is sitting in the seat of privilege, one is allowed to get away with more things or certain things are not looked upon as bad or are even bolstered and glorified in their favor. We see this when it comes to misogyny.

Of course, in a misogynistic society, women will be told to sex it up like a man! Some women have even convinced themselves they should have sex like a man and that it is to their benefit to do so. Again, to each their own, and this is an area for me that is still under transformation even as I write these words. I do not know where society is heading when it comes to this subject of women sexing like men. Again, I do believe these are male-dominant cues we are responding to. I also know that currently, and what I am seeing with myself and with other women, it is not the most beneficial for us to have sex like men. Understanding the value of our vaginas doesn't necessarily mean we put on a chastity belt in all cases, either. It means that we have to think critically about what we are doing with our vaginas and whom we are sharing it with, and how we are sharing it. We must think critically about what we really want and stop responding so blindly to these cues about sex and women.

Do we really want to have sex like a man? We can only think like a woman; again, I know what the books say about thinking like men. I question if we could ever understand the sexual mind of a human male as females.

This brings me to the topic of violence when it comes to sexual deviate behavior of men that goes even beyond misogyny. There is no topic more prevalent in human behavior than male violence against women, and yet, it is rarely discussed and is packaged as if it's a woman's problem. Men rarely hold each other accountable when it comes to misogyny and violence against women. You will hear men say things like, "Men should never hit a woman," well, even this is changing. And that's typically the extent of their revolution against violence towards women! But you will not see too many men taking a real stance against it. But with this said, we rarely see the demographic that benefits from something taking a real and substantial cause against it. This is why racism continues to exist, and this is why violence against women will continue, and the only demographic who can and will take a stand against it and make somewhat of a difference is the demographic who are being oppressed and being affected most by it. This, again, is why I believe as women, we must set the tone for how we are treated when it comes to our sexuality, our power and empowerment. And I just cannot see how sexing like a man can ever be to our benefit in this present-day climate.

Let's go and explore this a little deeper and how men really view sex and violence or how they are responding, at least. Let's delve into the true mind of a sexual human male. I am not saying here that all men will or are violent towards women, but a great number of them are. Too many of them are. By now, you all should know I'm not into statistics and charts, so go and look up the numbers for yourself on the rising account of violence against women in this country and even around the world. If a woman could really get in the mind of a man and understand his sexual mind and see it for herself, she would run to the nearest convent for shelter! And most honest men will tell you you do not want to know. There is no other perverse landfill than that of the sexual mind of the human male. Many men are even afraid of some of the sexual fantasies they have within and just will not go there. Thank God!

But there are many men who do act upon these fantasies, and they almost always involve pain and abuse to a woman and her sexually. We have convinced ourselves in this society (remember a male-dominant society) that the porn life should be mainstream and on display. Again, desensitization, which expresses that it is okay and "to each their own" to gang bang a woman, to fist a woman, to choke a woman to near unconsciousness, to urinate and defecate on a woman. People, this is not okay, and we should never normalize this behavior and laugh it off as something trivial. This is not victimless or crimeless. These are crimes against humanity. And it is and has found its way into our mainstream culture because we are blindly responding to those social cues in media. I have spoken to countless women who share about how their men are caught up in pornography and now want them to engage in these deviant sexual behaviors with them, and some women are, just to keep that man. Again, the more we accept this treatment, the more ingrained in our everyday society it becomes. Remember, porn 'stars' are simply prostitutes who agreed to be filmed; they are being paid to have sex with multiple people and in a voyorististic forum.

Women and men who engage in these sexually deviant behaviors are just as malfunctioning as the battered woman and male abuser relationship. Just because it's wrapped and cloaked in the idea of sex doesn't make it any less a form of abuse, and just because the person willingly participates doesn't make it any less a form of abuse. This is what desensitization does. I cannot say this enough. It normalizes behavior to the point of acceptance as true and right.

Now, mind you, I am not trying to get into folks' bedrooms. I'm trying to keep us out of folks' bedrooms. We do not need these images and behaviors on display in mainstream society as it is finding itself. I am certainly no prude, and as adults, we should be able to discuss sex and do what we want with our partners. But we also need to call things as they are, and any time one wants to bring pain and degradation to another human being, it is not right or true. I hear the moral police saying that's me putting my morality on someone else. Screw you! There should be some things deemed as wrong and right. A person who is allowing someone to urinate on them needs to know they are ill and the person who is doing it is sick as well. Now, I'm not naive enough to think we are going to stamp out these deviant behaviors. Hell, they have been around since the beginning of time. What I'm saying is that we are going in the wrong direction with normalizing it and displaying it as if it is okay.

My focus as to why I feel we need not normalize these things is because, as women, we will be the bearers of this continued abuse and violence, but instead of behind closed doors, it will become more and more acceptable in our general society, which is the case as I write these words even now.

I remember watching the movie Mr. and Mrs. Smith with Angelina Jolie and Brad Pitt. Now, yes, it's a movie. I kinda liked the movie, but I watched it with a critical eye and what the movie was saying to so many young women and men watching it. Brad Pitt's character was fighting his wife like she was a man and a stranger. Some of those scenes were very difficult for me to watch because I have worked with women who have been battered. The way he was fighting her should have killed her, but it barely fazed her, and she, in turn, was fighting him just as hard. But we know that the average woman's physical strength is not that of the average man. But what was most disturbing about the movie was the continued desire Mrs. Smith had for her husband, who was beating her. I thought the message this was sending was atrocious and mixed, to say the least, to the impressionable young folks in our country today. But hey, it's just a movie, right? I remember being at the gym running on the treadmill, and if your gym is like most these days, there are about 20 flat screens lined up. Talk about Matrix programming, but I digress. I remember seeing a TV movie premier that kept coming on over and over, and it was displaying on about 7 of those screens at the gym. I don't even remember what the movie title was, but I certainly remember the imagery. In the premiere, there was one scene that showed a man just cold cocking a woman and knocking her out unconscious, and it came on at least about 6 times in my run on that treadmill and displayed on those 7 screens, and everyone just went on about their business. Apparently, no one was phased that a man was knocking a woman out unconscious. Desensitization is a powerful tool.

This chapter is really about the transformation of the single independent woman and what our future may hold for us as independent women and as women begin to demand

129

more for ourselves. But to do this, we have to understand our culture and where we fit into it. We must understand things do not just form overnight; norms are developed and nourished. We cannot afford to continue to blindly respond to social cues that are degrading us and controlling our sexuality. Mirroring male sexuality is not the answer to combating this by any means. Our mirroring male sexuality has gotten us into the situations we are in today, from the bad advice of the 60s and thereon to our high divorce rates, high STD levels, unwanted pregnancies, broken homes, and mental health on the rise for women. This is what mirroring male sexuality has gotten us. We do not need to think like men; we need to think like women and act like women. Empower ourselves independently of men. When we "try" to think like a man, we continue to empower that man with authority over us because our quest is to please that man and male dominance. We must please ourselves first and foremost, do what is right for us, and not expect men to figure this out for us. They cannot! Men are just as blind and off-path as we are, and in many cases, even more. They are responding to those same social cues as well, except many of them are reaping the benefits of being allowed to keep a woman in a position of subjugation. Again, this is why big-time rappers get paid money to rap about sexually abusing a woman, and it's being blasted across our radio waves, and we are dancing to it. This is the reason why the white male-owned big music and movie producers continue to funnel funding into projects that support the debasement of women and keep women in a place of objectivity. It sells, and men buy into it the same as women.

As far as controversy goes, I have my ideals, ideas, and beliefs like the next person. I will passionately express them, as you know well by now. I'm not promoting that we all should think alike. I'm promoting critical thinking and questioning our laziness in just accepting things to be as it is fed to us. Me included. We all should be allowed to think and believe how we do. Challenging someone's beliefs is certainly fine, but putting people down and disassociating yourself from people because of their beliefs is a bullying tactic. I'm certainly not advocating that. If the person is respectful in indicating their beliefs, they must be accepted just as your beliefs are accepted. Who died and said you or I can be judge, jury and executioner? I will say that I am an unapologetically "judgemental" person. I happen to believe judging people can and is often a good thing and does benefit us. Now, executing people for their life decisions is another thing entirely. Judging means that you are taking into account that person and their decision-making skills, behaviors, and actions while forming your own opinion about them. I believe that is quite a fair approach, and it is what most people do. It's just PC to say that we do not "judge" people. *insert rolled eyes and sigh here.

Everything I say in this book is my opinion, and people can choose to agree or not. This doesn't mean my opinions are right and true, no more than anyone else's. Controversial viewpoints can and often cause dissension and strife. It just comes with the nature of what it is. Going against the grain is painful for all parties. If one person can say they like to lick someone's ass, then I can say I do not, and that's nasty in my book. That's not judging anyone or being intolerant. Just as you voiced your viewpoints, so did I. If we could grasp a hold of this concept, the world would truly be a better place. That disagreement does not mean we have to become adversaries or enemies. It's just that we see things differently, and we can still exist in the same space together as we choose to be. There are a lot of things I have an opinion on or just don't see the logic behind it, but that does not mean I hate the people who represent that or that I want them to come to some unfortunate demise. That's ridiculous. We are all human beings at the end of the day. We all have a right to be who we want as long as it does not hurt anyone else who may be unable to protect themselves. If what you are doing is causing harm to another living being (like an animal) who is unable to protect themselves or a person who does not have the mental capabilities to protect themselves. We need to understand the difference between controversy and real harm. Some things just disrupt our sensibilities because we may not understand why people do those things; okay then, give your opinion and move the hell on. And then there are some things that are a detriment to human well-being, like someone who goes into a crowded room and yells fire that causes people to be trampled to death. Okay, now those people need to be locked up for a spell.

For example, speaking of controversy, lesbians. That was a great segue. I have never understood why lesbians can be the stereotypical "butchy" lesbian. When I think of the concept of women loving on women, I think of the most feminine of all creatures. Like when two lesbians walk in the room, daffodils follow in their footsteps or some shit like that. I know that's going into the gender role of things and who gets to assign gender roles. In my opinion, women, in general, are more feminine than men. We like pretty things and aesthetically see the world differently. Why any woman would want to be or act like a man is beyond me (a man as defined by American culture). If anything, I think the butchy lesbians are responding to a male dominant society and taking cues from society that says that in order to love a woman, I must act like a man. That just makes no sense to me whatsoever. I mean, if I was a lesbian and did not want a man, why would I want a woman who looks and acts like a man? Again, things that make me go, hmmmm? These are my opinions, and they may have just disrupted your sensibilities, but has what I just said caused real human harm? It shouldn't have. I will go even further. This is why I love those lipstick lesbians. They are the ones not responding to gender assignments and male-dominant cues. I feel that a woman who embraces her femininity and loves a woman romantically is stating that she can only be who she was created to be, which is a woman. Why should a woman have to turn her back on her femininity just because she decides to love another woman? Do I have my beliefs about lesbianism altogether? Yes, I do, but they're my beliefs, just as lesbians have their beliefs, and every individual person has their beliefs, opinions, and thoughts. Who is right, and does it matter? I am certainly not here to execute anyone. I do not have a heaven or hell to put anyone. We should still be able to love people even when we disagree with their lifestyles. We should be able to interact with people with respect and dignity and want the best for them because they are human beings. Oh yes, I can hear the Christian community talking about their rhetoric of stumbling blocks and supporting people and their sins. Well, Christian men and women, you lie every day. Should I stop socializing with you? Should I not come and attend your lying ass wedding ceremony because I know you slept with that man/woman before your last divorce was even final? Oops! Yes, we are good about trying to condemn people and forget the shit we do or did. We all have a right to live as we choose, and we all have a right to believe what we want.

So, this is where opinions and controversy get folks in trouble. Because their own sensibilities are disrupted, and they have a difficult time processing what someone else is saying, a need may arise in them to shut that person down. But if we allow people to be shut down because they express a difference in opinion and live their lives a certain way, then EVERYONE must be shut down. Who is Right? Again, being mindful that what people are expressing and doing does not cause harm to those who cannot readily defend themselves.

Even though I was making a point about controversy, opinions and what constitutes real human harm (or, in my opinion, should at least), there is a place where lesbians fit in with this whole independent woman scene. Well, there are plenty of lesbians who are independent women, and there are many who are not. Most independent women get accused of being lesbians on the regular because, again, a woman shouldn't be so assertive or independent, for that matter, from men, and again, the misconstruing of assertive energy as masculine energy. Yet again, we find ourselves grappling with the complexity of gender roles and expectations that persist even when we believe we are taking a stand against them. While I appreciate certain defined roles, I also advocate for a more nuanced understanding of these roles. It is advantageous for women to distance ourselves from some of those traditional definitions simply because many of these traditional definitions were flawed and rooted in male privilege from the outset.

I was being a bit facetious above when I gave the analogy of lesbians walking into the room with daffodils following behind them. The point I am making is that as women, we should be comfortable in our femininity and accept it as such, and we should not have to apologize for being girly, feminine and a bulldog just the same when it comes to other matters of assertion. Being a feminine woman also means being accepted as a viable partner, an equal. And yes, as women, we do have a scale of femininity. Some of us are more feminine than others, and that is okay. And some even "Butchy," I will give you that my butchy lesbian sisters or heterosexual sister who is just testosteroney like that. I don't believe it's necessary or any more natural than being just a feminine-acting woman. I can accept it and love you still at the end of the day, especially if you are in my circle of support.

There's this belief that males and masculinity have somehow gotten things correctly, and I just think nothing can be further from the truth. That somehow taking on the persona of male energy, "wearing the pants," strutting instead of switching like a woman, wearing plaid and work boots, somehow gives us credibility as "strong" women. I think that's pretty shitty thinking. I like my floral skirts and strappy heels. I think we need to wear more floral skirts and heels when conducting business. If some dumb ass guy is distracted by our flowers, that's his F-ing issue. We shouldn't have to hide our femininity because men can't control themselves, to cover up what makes us women, which is our femininity. I'm not saying go to work with your asses and boobs out; that's the feminist agenda; burn your bras. No, there is something called common sense, and there is such a thing as being unnecessarily distracting. But a woman who expresses her femininity with her hair, wearing a good bra and a skirt to show off her ankles, so the hell what! I am still an equal and can conduct myself in a professional manner, and you will accept me as such. Women shouldn't have to "man up" to feel on equal grounds with men. This is why I love hearing powerful women speak, like Oprah, Dr. Frances Cress Welsing, Goldie Hawn, Michelle Obama,

Diane Sawyer, Dr. Joy Degruy Leary, and so many more. These women are just the epitome of femininity to me. Women who have been able to maintain their femininity and power at the same time. They embrace their femininity and allow it to lead them, and do not apologize for it. And when these women speak, people listen, and their intellect is unmatched.

This line of thinking is also the reason why I will never celebrate Caitlyn Jenner as a woman. Now that's a controversial topic! I could give two shits if Caitlyn had become a green person, let alone a woman. I have been a woman for 50 years, as many have been all our lives, and we have never been celebrated for just being a woman. But a man can come along who has been in the seat of privilege not only one seat but several seats with being a Wealthy-White-Male for all his life, and now I am supposed to celebrate him because he had a surgery? Hell no! This man has not experienced the life of a woman and what that truly entails. He got to where he is today from being a privileged man! It upsets me that it took a man to "become a woman" in order to somehow inform society of how great being a woman is.

Male dominance delusions at its best! Toxic Masculinity at its best! And we bought it and still are. So, until we start choosing just random, everyday women and lifting them up in celebration just because they are women, I will not celebrate any man becoming a woman just because he can afford a fucking surgery! There's no bravery in that, in my opinion. You see, he didn't clip those nuts of his because as soon as he stops taking any hormones or whatever else he takes, he will revert to being a man, just in case he doesn't like this woman thing. GTFOH!!

Now, where I will celebrate Bruce Jenner (and is there a name more masculine than Bruce! LOL..I digress) is in the act of not cutting off those nuts of his and his expression of still wanting to be with a woman, and I'm going to tell you why. Let the controversy continue. Now, I know that Catelyn is evolving as I write these words, so to be honest, I am not sure where he is in his transition, but where Bruce Jenner has made an impact is in gender description. Clothing and masculine/feminine energy (as culturally defined) does not entirely define who a woman or man is. I believe a woman and man are defined within the core of our spirits and what we were designed to be as procreators. What is the DNA? Men have a penis to procreate, and women, a vagina/womb! And I happen to believe that designation happened way before we even got here to this present-day consciousness. However, I will save that topic for another writing endeavor. Therefore, I do not believe wearing a dress with frills should be an issue for a woman in power and that we should wear those dresses that enhance our breasts! We are women! Or a woman wearing combat boots and a buzz cut doesn't make her any more masculine. When we sit down and contemplate the concept of gender, clothing, etc., it absolutely makes no sense. A female is a woman physiologically/biologically, and a male is a man physiologically/biologically; there is no denying this, and this must be respected. I do not give a damn what the transgender people say and do! Do your boo, and I will do me. However, we BOTH must be allowed to do so. No one has any more rights over anyone else to their own opinions and beliefs. You do not get the right to tell me how I am supposed to view someone, and neither do I. Yes, as I mentioned, we can and should be able to express ourselves in culturally feminine or masculine ways, and often, we do this with our outer appearance. We do because our perception is that it may be appealing to the opposite gender or the person whom we are trying to attract. There are also still social norms to respect and follow if we desire a particular outcome. Some want to thumb their noses at these norms but then complain about not receiving the results they wanted. They are called rules and expectations for a reason, and there will always be a need to uphold rules and expectations as a means to a certain end.

Now, society pushes us in a certain direction when we express ourselves in certain ways. Oh, she's butchy, or he's faggoty or a sissy because of how the person is expressing and what results quite often is we start identifying with those societal cues and acting on them. I happen to think some people are just more feminine or masculine than others, quite possibly due to physiological reasons of estrogen and testosterone levels. I happen to think I am a woman with more testosterone than the average woman. I am still very much attracted to males and the dick, though.

I believe outer expression with clothing and posturing becomes more than what it needs to be, and a type of confusion forms. This is why we have many Lesbians who do dress butchy or act "manly" and will even utilize strap-on penises with their female partners…WTH? I can speculate. This is also why Chris Jenner has decided to keep his man joystick. The pussy feels good to the joystick, and the dick feels good to the pussy. Point… Blank… Period. They were designed for each other! If you do not want the dick, then why go there. Well, we go there because that attraction to the opposite gender physically and sexually is still there. There is no denying this, but it's not something we talk about because we want an easy answer regarding these gender roles and laws of attraction, sex organs, who defines these things and what they really mean in relation to human organisms, or we do not want to offend anyone because they have chosen a certain lifestyle. Asking questions and thinking critically should never offend anyone. Trying to figure out why we do the things we do should never offend anyone. I do not have any definitive answers myself. I certainly do not believe the attraction to the opposite gender or same gender is just about sex either. That's not what I'm indicating at all. What I challenge women to do is to question why they do the things they do. Why am I trying to imitate "masculine energy" "Why am I using a strap-on when I have said I do not want a man? Is this truly the case, or am I responding to societal cues or from a place I have not explored within?" So, these are my opinions on some of the issues of female controversies within our culture. And if you were to ask my opinion about all of this, I'd say do like Caitlyn Jenner and keep the dick or the pussy and just play dress up with your partner. I wouldn't even suggest going as far as Caitlyn Jenner did with having life-threatening surgeries, either. And even though I question some of these issues with gender, clothing, and sexuality as they relate to women, I still can respect women and their decisions to do as they please. I would even go as far as to tell that butchy woman to dress how she wants and find her man who likes to play dress up as well, and then they can live happily ever after with no strap-ons and share each other's strappy heels! I would suggest starting there first before responding to social cues that suggest you do not want the dick or the pussy. They truly were made for each other. Let's remember even the Pharaohs of antiquity wore mini skirts and strappy sandals, and even Jesus wore a long duster gown. Sex, Gender and Clothing should have no relation to femininity and masculinity; however, it does, and because it does, we can give it some perspective respect. JMHO ((Shrugs)).

These are my controversial opinions and thoughts on the subject matter of being an independent woman in today's culture and what that can mean from many different angles, from being a feminine, independent woman, to being a butchy lesbian independent woman, to being a single black woman to being a Cougar, and even to being a woman who uses her sex organs for monetary gain. As women, we will be unfairly judged by males and by each other. Even I have judgments about what it means to be a woman, and guess what? This is okay. It's controversial, it's provocative, but it is okay. Anything to do with our vaginas is controversial because, again, there is a male perspective and desire to control it and us. It is a deep-seated desire that is truly out of the faultiness of being a human being. People like controlling each other, and minorities are always in a vulnerable position just because our demographic does not hold as much power or perception of power. This should not deter us from self-defining our own feminine realities of what we want out of this life. What I challenge women to do with all this information is to step back and ask themselves: is this something that is of benefit to me and my womanhood, or am I quite possibly responding to male-dominant cues to dictate my reality? I do believe there is a gravitation that women do towards that which is male-oriented, and in our minds, this becomes more valid than feminine. I want to dispel these beliefs within us as women. We can be valid and a force and still celebrate our femininity. As stated earlier in this chapter and others, should women obtain a collective mindset of change, there will quite possibly be a backlash of more pressure and even more from those male-dominant social norms. Preparing ourselves for this and pushing back against it in whatever form that may mean for us as women is critical. I can foresee future parallels to the series "The Handmaid's Tale." A series that I had to stop watching because it rang with too much truth and a reality that could become very real for us as women. I have enough mistrust about males that a series such as that just sends me over the edge. I do believe things may get worse before they get better. However, there is work that can be done to bring attention to these very feminine issues. Whether it means protesting in our communities, having town meetings, going into meetings with our legislators to press the issue of women's rights and fairness across the board, developing and organizing with each other in our workplaces and careers, writing a book, blogging or being a Facebook activist, whatever platform we have, we must speak out and share about these discrepancies that attack our birthright as born women.

We will not see change until we change it and change our minds about what is of benefit to us from a feminine perspective rather than a male-dominant perspective. We do not have to imitate male dominance to be a force of reckoning.

Last Chapter:
No Answers…Suggestions Only!!

Okay, have you shaken off the last chapter yet? Let's get back to this single-woman circus. All along, you have been saying all the good ones are taken or married. You were right! For the most part, they are, but there is a small percentage of men who are still out there and who are right for you. Does this mean we are doomed, that we are to live a life of singlehood forever?

No, but we have to realize by the time guys have cycled through a few relationships, they are 'damaged goods,' as are we since we have been through our various relationships also. So, we have a few bruises, but that doesn't mean we are not edible, like a ripened fruit. It may be a little mushy, but it still has a good taste and some nutrients. We've been knocked around by the love suitcase. Packing and unpacking all that trauma, just to repack it again and try moving up the street. After a while, anyone would be confused about which direction and road they are supposed to take. What we learn and accept is either we are going to be alone or we will have to help folks unpack some of their emotional luggage. Accept some of those bruises and try to make a dish from it. It can be something there that's salvageable. And possibly even better.

In this chapter, I will make suggestions to the everyday, average woman and women who want to become more independent and find some contentment within themselves on being single and independent. These same women also have hope of maintaining a relationship with a good male of the human species on this planet of nearly 8 billion people. I have already told you, ladies, there are no definitive answers now. It never has been. We must figure this out for ourselves, our lives, and our sanity. In this chapter, I hope to summarize some key points from the previous chapters in one last attempt to help myself as well as any (aspiring) independent woman reading this. It is just one last-ditch effort for us to wizen up and learn to play smarter.

As women, we are bullheaded, and we just cannot keep blaming men for the "things" they are doing or not doing for us in relationships. Yes, I started this book in a personal vent, and yes, I am still angry about how callous we all have become when it comes to matters of the heart. How haphazard we have become regarding other beings whom we say we care about. This does anger me. But what I have learned and continue to learn, or better yet, accept. Is that no one can do anything to me that I do not allow? Yes, it's an old cliché but a tried and true one. And, the more mess I allow, the more messed up the dating canvas becomes.

We can no longer allow men to set the standards for us. We can no longer allow them to designate and initiate what we will and will not do. We can no longer look to a man to approve or disapprove of us. Their assessment tools are just not adequate for this and probably have never been. We didn't have too many choices over the years but to survive in a sense. Yes, our society is still very much patriarchal, but with that said, this doesn't mean we have to continue to accept those male-dominated cues. That's pointing us in the direction that favors them. We are still teaching our daughters and girls they are to please a man, dumb themselves down, and sex themselves up to be accepted. All the while, our daughters and girls have very little protection against the predators that are roaming around looking for their next victim. At least back in the day, a young girl had her brothers and father who would go and fight for her honor if a man sexed her up and left her. Back in the day, the "shotgun wedding," as noted in a previous chapter, was real. A girl's male Kinfolk wasn't having it if a man came and sexed up their sister or daughter and got her pregnant; they went after that man and made him marry that woman with a gun pointed at his back while he said, "I do." Some of us wish our fathers and brothers would go after some of these pervs and could get away with shooting them. But again, the laws are there to not only protect us but also to protect the pervs, lucky sonsabitches.

To be honest, who wants to be forced into a relationship with a coward of a man as the shotgun weddings so often did for women? It's not so much that the law protects us from pervs these days but rather abuse. It shouldn't be a surprise that women have suffered and still do at the hands of men in more than one way, and we are still fighting for protective laws that send clear and definite punishment to men who do abuse women. However, a man hoeing around is not abuse by any means that needs protection under the law, unfortunately! This brings me to another point: when a man is hoeing around on you, that's when our own personal laws must be declared. If you do not want to be in a relationship with a man cheating on you, then why are you? It still befuddles me the number of women who forgive a cheating man not once but numerous times. Yes, I believe in working through things; if you are in a committed relationship, give the other person the benefit of the doubt to make it right, but they must take on that responsibility. When you are constantly forgiving egregious acts like cheating time after time, then you are the one taking on that responsibility. You are the one enabling that person to continue in their ways. Just leave otherwise, do not complain. You have absolutely no one to blame but yourself for allowing someone to stay in your space who is mistreating you.

As women, we have more options now. We can be smarter and play smarter instead of ending up with a cheating man, unwanted pregnancies, STDs, being labeled a hoe, and in financial ruin because we hold the erroneous belief a man is going to save us somehow. We save ourselves now! We can't depend on a man to form our definitions of who we are. If we did that, we would continue to be in this state of confusion because where one man will tell you he likes your independence, another man may not. We would drive ourselves crazy trying to keep up with the changing demands, as many of us are doing right now.

Don't get me wrong; I want to be able to rely on a man but also give myself some time to know that man is trustworthy. There are some predators out there who absolutely hate women and what the woman stands for. Men who will say everything a woman wants to hear until he gets what he wants from her, which is typically some ass, and then he's gone. A man we are dating or seeing can never be that man we trust to lean on because there is no real test of commitment there. Commitment is formed over time. And just because someone says they are committed to you doesn't mean they are. This is one I had to learn the hard way a couple of different times and ways. I am a conscientious person myself; I tend to think most people are like me. And when I tell a man I'm in it with him, and I want to make this work, and I am there for him. 95% of the time,

I mean it. But some people can lie to your face repeatedly. If you are a person of integrity and who knows yourself, you must come to the realization that not everyone has journeyed to that kind of self-discovery and decency. Yes, it still catches me off guard how self-centered people can be, but if we are to safeguard our hearts and minds, we should come to this conclusion. We must think critically when it comes to a man who hasn't been in our lives long. Do not start to become too dependent on that man too quickly, emotionally, financially, or otherwise. Again, commitment is formed over time and the investing of time. Never allot to a man responsibility that you could not do by yourself and on your own, especially at the beginning of a relationship. There are no guarantees that any man will stay with you forever. Even after 20 to 30 years of marriage, men are leaving, as are women. This is the nature of our society today. Never get yourself in situations you cannot get out of by yourself. Stop getting yourselves into these large mortgages with men, spouses or otherwise. Do we really need every upgrade we see on HGTV? If we cannot afford a home with just our income, then we do not need to be in that home. Who knows what could happen to your significant other other than just leaving you? He could become injured and cannot work, possibly even die. Again, we must stop buying into these fantasy lives, Barbie and her dream home. Currently, it benefits us to think about downsizing and not upgrading unless, again, you can afford these upgrades with just one income. If it is a home you want, ladies, then purchase that home on your own and have it coming into your relationship and never put that man legally on that home you bought. Keep it in your family and under your family name, and never sell that home to purchase another home with your man. Now, if the two of you want to Co-invest in a nonresidential home, that's cool beans as well. And if you want to move into a home a man already owns, and he pays for, that's even better; you keep your home as rental property. Again, these are suggestions, as there are no definitive answers. Our finances need to be at the forefront of our thoughts, not on the back burner. We are still caught up in the days of old of our finances merging with the man and becoming his finances. No! There was a time when women could not manage their own finances, and what we had just automatically went to our husbands. Hell to the motherfucking nawl, not anymore! And although the laws have changed, we are still under the mindset of merging finances with men and becoming one. I know I hear the alarm bells going off in your little lady heads saying, "But we are one," "he is my man," "We are in this together." Ladies, you can still fully support your man's interests and goals and even help him financially if you so choose without merging finances with that man LEGALLY. There is absolutely nothing that is taken away from your relationship just because you choose to manage your own money, assets, and finances. That is a sensitivity that men have and that we have covered throughout this book of men not fully accepting women as having more than them or being more financially stable than they are coming into the relationship. That sounds like a personal problem to me that they must get over. I would even go as far as to say it's more beneficial for you both not to combine your incomes legally anyway; the government has ways of programming us in their favor. And I will leave that one alone to another writing endeavor. Now, if you choose to allow your man to take care of you and be the breadwinner, more power to you and good luck with that. I am not saying that women should or have to work outside the home, but remember the reality of our society, where the divorce rate is 40% - 50%. Would you get into a moving vehicle if they told you there was a 50% chance it would crash? Hmmmm? I'm just stating facts here. It won't happen to you, right? Well, that's what we all said, and look at our asses now! Not all of us can make a career out of being a baby mama, and remember that child support does stop after a certain age. Hey, I do not make the rules. I am just reporting what's trending now. If you want to be at the mercy of what that man can give you and how much, then that's your prerogative, but you have no one to blame if things do not work in your favor and you have no skills or assets to fall back on for yourself if your relationship does come to an end. If you do want to be a stay-at-home mom and raise your children, I think that is a great and noble cause, and I am an advocate for stay-at-home mothers and fathers who want to have one parent in the home with the younger children. But with this said, be thinking about self-development and educate yourself. Participate in online classes or night classes as the children get older; get a part-time job in your field of study. Well, that sounds like a woman preparing to leave her husband and family; yes, I heard that in your lady mind or male mind. That line of thinking is a male-dominated line of thinking and a male chauvinist line of thinking. Again, a woman developing herself is just that. She may want to enter the workforce and be competitive one day, or she may have to due to a spousal injury, layoff, or a failed relationship. Preparing ourselves for the worst is a human right, and you better if you want to survive. Relying on a man to be the only one preparing for a rainy day is you and him being dumbassey. Get smart, ladies!

Another suggestion I have is that we stop taking on the burden of why men leave or stay, as suggested in a previous chapter. It's that man's choice whether he leaves or stays, and there is nothing we can do about it. That is his responsibility, his loyalty, and his commitment level. Women leave just as men do, and oftentimes, women will suggest a divorce or initiate leaving physically first. But in many of these cases, the man has already left her emotionally alone. Men have mastered emotionally leaving us, pushing us away until we have no other choice but to leave physically. I still believe that a woman will stay with her man way longer than a man stays with his woman emotionally. And a man will stay with a woman physically longer than a woman will stick around. I was going to insert some bullshit statistic here to support this claim but really, read up on it for yourselves. Is it any real wonder why a man sticks around physically with us and has checked out on us emotionally? Yes, you guessed it, to get some free, clean coochie, as well as financial reasons. There may be some love there or feelings, but it's more of a dependent love than a voluntary, giving and investing type of love. In the case I reference here, the two of you have stopped growing. Often, in situations like this, the relationship has stagnated. We must start seeing and calling these relationship breakdowns for what they are. Many people stay with each other out of very selfish or even practical reasons rather than love. There are people who stay with each other and are afraid of each other; that one day, the other may do something to them violently, but they still stay. It is dysfunctional at its best. Many women who find themselves in situations like this are the women who have allowed themselves to become too dependent on that man, and often, it's due to finances and security. They do not want to lose their lifestyle their home, but will forsake their sanity, safety and even the growth of their children by keeping them in a toxic environment.

Again, I'm not suggesting women just leave their men at the drop of adversity. I'm referring to abuse and when a relationship is beyond repair or at least one or both parties are not willing to work on making things better. If you are at odds with each other to the point of not talking, sleeping in separate bedrooms, not seeing each other for days, and there's suspicion of cheating. That is toxicity at its best. That is not a relationship. I do not believe in people staying together at all costs. In relationships like this, we literally can lose our sanity and will engage in crimes against each other. There are how many seasons of the TV shows "Snapped" and "Forensic Files?" Need I say more? But, I will, of course. When a person is behaving in ways that indicate they are no longer respecting you or honoring their commitment to you, then it's time to consider a separation or end of that relationship. Especially if they are ignoring tools to help the relationship get back on track. In addition to losing your sanity, keeping children in toxic environments where parents are warring with each other is probably one of the worst things people can do to their children. You are now modeling for your children how to be just as dysfunctional in their future relationships. I have always believed that an absent parent is better than a dysfunctional parent. I'm all for two-parent households and folks raising their children together. But suppose you cannot raise your children together and show your children what a good functioning relationship is. In that case, it is best for that child to experience both parents in separate environments. So, if that man wants to leave, then let him. If a separation is in order for just a while, then do what you must and then come back together with a plan of improving the relationship. When you are not so dependent on that man, financially, emotionally, or otherwise, you will not forsake your sanity and children to "keep" that man. I also believe that when people understand the other person is not so dependent on them and can function outside of them, they are more apt to respect each other. It is not your responsibility to keep a man! Only animals should be kept on a leash. Sorry ladies, its not legal yet to install invisible electric fencing for your men to stay in your yard. And no flavor of Milkshakes will bring them back either! So, until then, we must let them go if they are disrespecting us, the family, and our children. And, if you have your shit together, you will be okay when he does.

Another suggestion to women is to stop having children with men who have shown them to be irresponsible men. BOOM! If a man is not taking care of the children he had before the one he had with you, there's nothing to hold on to that he will take care of yours. This is another complaint I hear from women about the "no good ass man" who won't come and spend time with his child, will not help them financially with the child, and basically doesn't want anything to do with the child. But that woman failed to tell us that the man had two other children that he half saw, didn't really pay anything to care for them, and the children were barely one years old before he "got" her pregnant. Ladies... Ladies! Tsk Tsk! We cannot blame that man! That was all you. Okay, say that man didn't tell you he had other children; how long did you get to know him before you had unprotected sex? Yes, that's a touchy one, isn't it? I have been there also and was doing the happy Jesus dance after that trip to Walgreens, too! But this is the thing, ladies, we make these decisions that can be life-altering. We don't want to admit to them or just live in denial about them, but we are doing these things to ourselves with these men we are entering sexual relationships with too quickly.

We want to be loved so desperately, and in a relationship with a man that we allow ourselves to be exposed to all kinds of things we do not want; again, the unwanted pregnancies,

STDs, premature emotional bonding with a man who may not even be in it with us for more than 3 months. We want that Barbie dream, the fantasy that somehow, we will change that man. He will become this miraculously wonderful man with us because we are special. You got the good coochie! You pretty! Your makeup is slaying. And I love how the men will even convince some of these women they are special with that goodie good, tell them they love them in the first week of knowing them, and we believe them! The love bombers. These men even singing songs about it. And the same men singing these songs are cheating on their women! Why aren't we catching on to these shenanigans? We want to believe these men so desperately. Well, ladies, some of this is just how we were made. How we are made up emotionally as women. As women, we thrive and do very well in committed and loving relationships, and we feel most like ourselves when we are in one. And that's all fine and good; nature knows what is best. But we have veered away significantly from what nature wants for us in the form of relationships in our present-day culture. And not to get too religious and spiritual on y'all, but it's also common-sense realities instilled into our being that are quite physiological. Science, really. There is a science behind some of this craziness that we feel towards a man whom we have engaged with sexually. I briefly mentioned it in a previous chapter, and it's called Oxytocin. This is a hormone that we all have, men and women, but women tend to use it most efficiently. It's called the bonding or cuddle hormone, as it's released abundantly when a mother nurses her child. This hormone helps the mother to bond to her child in that visceral protective way we mothers tend to do. Well, this hormone is also released when we have an orgasm with a man. Starting to make a bit more sense now, ladies? Yes, when a woman has sex with a man and orgasms, she feels a stronger sense of attachment to that man, and women produce more of this hormone than men do. So, it's no wonder why we go batshit crazy for a man after he starts giving us good dick. These physiological facts must be considered when dealing with men. We need to educate ourselves on just being a woman, the type of woman we are, and the type of woman we want to be. I know there are plenty of women still out there who believe they can think and act like a man, and hey, if it's working for you, I hope you have fun. But for me, I know myself, and once I start giving my body to a man, I'm in it with that man because, for one, I value my body and sexual nature as something that is special and should only be shared with a man who is special to me. I cannot deny the facts of the physiological pulls towards that man after sex. But this is what I do not understand with women who do engage with men on "just" a sexual level. Many of these women become very hateful towards men. And make the most obtuse comments about men and how they sex them and leave them. It's as if they are angry with men in general. Oh, I thought you were having fun with sexing and leaving that man, Sis? What's the problem? The men sure as hell don't seem to be having any problems with sexing and leaving you. But if you listen closely to these women who are in "relationships" or, better yet, situationships with these men, they also have complaints about that man and what he is doing and not doing regarding them. Oh, I thought this was "just" a sexual relationship. How can you get mad or put demands on a man with whom you are just having sex with? That man owes you something other than sex? Hmmmm, that's interesting. Well, my conclusion to this is that these women obviously want more than sex from these men but have tried to convince themselves otherwise and that they are okay with nothing more than sex, and when this little minor detail is brought up to these women, they will justify to the ends of the earth in defense of why they are staying in these sexual relationships. Trust and believe; it is just a sexual relationship for that man. And therein lays the difference between men and women. In the woman's mind, someday, that man is going to change his feelings towards her and give her more. But when this doesn't happen, and this woman is continuously having sex with this man at his beck and call, and he is not investing more in her, she becomes angry with that man. Now, all men are like the last man. It is likely that this woman has had other relationships like this with other men and has come out on the short end of the stick even then, no pun intended. Often, that woman will remain in that situation with that man for years and wait for him to "get it together" for her. All the while trying to convince herself this is something she is in control of and wants. Disappointment settles in when that man never commits and moves on to the next woman. Often committing to the next woman who had higher standards, boundaries and expectations. As mentioned, many women who claim they just want to have sex with men and leave them are angry for the very reason why they are sexing with the man and "leaving" him. Because they have been left numerous times when they had sexed with a man or invested more into him when he was just having sex and it was all he ever wanted. They feel used and then, in turn, want to use men. Hurt them and get back at them. Our minds can justify almost anything to us so that we can be comfortable with the decisions we make. Not to get too scholarly here, but it's called Cognitive Dissonance, which is basically a state of having inconsistent thoughts, beliefs and attitudes that relate to our behavior. And again, it's your life. Do you as the quotes are saying. I have a gripe because women with these mindsets are making it more difficult for us women, who admit we want more from men in a relationship than just sex.

On to the next suggestion, if a man tells you he loves you within the first week or two of knowing him, my suggestion: DO NOT BELIEVE HIM!! I know you gals are ready to burn this damn book down to the ground NOW. Reality hurts, doesn't it? Bless your hearts.

I know, again, I have been there. Surely, if someone tells you they love you, they must mean it. Okay, I will give the fellas a little bit of a break here and even you ladies because we so want to believe this. I think people may say they love someone early on because they really really do want to believe it. And it's not that they are trying to mislead or lie (of course, there are the douches out there that do lie intentionally), but I believe that most people say this because they want it so badly. But it's just not true DOT COM!

I'm going to tell you why it's not true. Love forms over time. Commitment forms over time. 1-2 weeks of knowing someone is not enough time to grow into love with them, and I will add, for most people. A person's love levels and commitment levels go hand in hand. You cannot have one without the other. I believe commitment keeps people around longer than love.

Therefore, we are seeing the revolving door of the serial dating that's going on. People are flying into relationships so quickly and saying they love each other and are committed to each other and have yet to even have their first argument with each other. Have yet to allow the reality of who they really are to settle on the other person. I have heard so many people complain about how someone could tell them they loved them last week, but this week, they are out the door because of a petty disagreement. Reality check: they never loved them from the beginning.

If someone tells you they love you in the first week or so, month even. My suggestion is to tell them that you need more time, and if they can't handle this and want to pressure you on the topic of loving them after a week, then maybe that is not the person for you. I had a man whom I had only spoken to over the phone, no dates, and had not even met in person. This man tried to convince me to accept him as "My Man" just from our phone conversations. Motherfuckah, please!! But these are the types of things going on in our dating and single world these days. We want things so yesterday and are not willing to put in the work necessary to keep it for tomorrow. And our culture is very much a culprit in these microwave relationships that we want to cook fast! We want to get to the happily ever after, the desert before the 5-course meal. We want to build a skyscraper when we haven't even poured the concrete foundation yet. Much of this is just because we have so much access to each other. We have numerous means of communication that can make us feel close to each other. I went over this in-depth in the previous chapter on social media. You would think with all this access to each other, we would be happier and fulfilled, but I honestly believe we are lonelier and separated from each other even more. This, again, instigates within a person to want that love so badly that they are willing to fabricate it in their minds. We have access to each other but in very non-personal mediums, social media being a huge one, texting, etc. We can spend hours upon hours with people online, and our minds can trick us into thinking we strongly care about them. And that's not to say we don't have a type of care for them, but it is not love. It's not love in the sense that you really know that person and have had personal experiences with them. And even after a few dates with someone, face to face, love is most likely not established even then. Sometimes, it takes years to grow in love with another person. I'm speaking about the type of love that is long-lasting and unconditional. Now, again, people do have different love levels. I do not think love means the same thing to every person, but there are some concrete things about love that are agreeable to most people and can be seen with the eye in how people treat each other. And I will add another disclaimer here: I do believe that people can form strong bonds with each other through online, phone conversations, etc. I do believe that even strong relationships can and have come from limited medium interactions if both parties are mature and have good intentions toward each other. But again, we just must take that time to ensure the authenticity of those feelings. And those feelings can grow more robust and into love once you start to share personal face-to-face experiences with one another. I'm just cautioning you to be leery of a man telling you he loves you after a couple of dates or before you even meet. That man is likely confused, lonely and/or possibly on that agenda to get you in bed quickly because men know that a woman who feels in love with a man will give up the ass quickly as well. The Douche 101, which I have also covered thoroughly. Hands up, you have been warned.

My next suggestion regards an old and tried dynamic of male and female relations. It involves the oldest "profession" on the planet. The act of using sex as a means of gain in other areas. I like to refer to this as Hoe-ify. Pronounced: Hoe-ah-fi... long I. It's not prostitution itself but mimics it in a sense. At least with prostitution, they really are getting paid. They are getting something out of it instead of just a wet and sore ass. My definition of Hoe-ify is when a woman allows a man to reduce her to just her vagina and tits, debase her as an object to be lusted after, and most importantly, that woman believes there's value to this debasement and therefore she excuses it as something that will bring her gain.

Ladies, do you ever wonder why there is not a viable industry of male strip clubs and male whore houses. Think about that for a minute. Yes, there are male strippers and prostitutes. But think about the last time you saw men patrolling the street as hookers and when was the last time you been in an ALL male strip club (brick and mortar) building that is open every day, every week, year after year. Right, not very many are there? Now, let's recall the umpteen million female strip clubs across our country, as well as the zillion female prostitutes who patrol the city streets and back alleys. Why do you think this is? Well, there is another reason other than men being far more sexually perverted than women. The main reason is that men don't have to engage, or at least society says he does not on this sexual level, to gain something in return. He does the debasement; he is not the debased. Again, it comes down to women being too dependent on that which is male-oriented, orchestrated and manipulated. We are blindly responding to male dominance and what men want, and unfortunately, there are far too many women who will acquiesce with little thought to how this affects women as a whole. No woman has to be a prostitute or stripper. But leave it up to Hollywood, pop culture and mass media (very male-oriented industries). Being a prostitute or stripper is something that should be celebrated, glorified and uplifted. They will say it's the liberated woman who engages in these things because she can, again, sex like a man, and women believe this lie. But the reality is that a woman's sexuality can be controlled by men and reduced to an object to be exploited. That is when we lose more of our control over ourselves and our own sexuality. There is absolutely nothing wrong with a woman expressing her sexuality and being herself, but we must analyze why we are doing the things we do for ourselves. As I have mentioned before, I am far from a prudish woman. I am a very sexual and sensual woman; however, I have boundaries and parameters that I live my life within, and I'm not here to try to place my parameters on others, which is why I have titled this chapter as "suggestions." These are my suggestions. You can either take it or leave it. That's your right. But do try to recall the discrepancies in how men express sexually and how women express sexually. Why is it that men can remain fully clothed, and women are sexualized? Because they can and do. And we can also, but instead, many of us just take the easy way out. Women have found it to be lucrative to get what they want by using their sexuality, and favors will be bestowed upon that woman by certain men. That is the reality of it. But the question then becomes, at what expense? At the expense of teaching our daughters and young women, they should dumb themselves down and debase themselves sexually if it gets the male attention they crave and monetary gain. Recall the chapter on the Barbie clone syndrome, where women, young and old, are self-mutilating just to fit a mode that is male-made and orchestrated. At the expense of all women being steadily short-changed because we are just not engaging on an intellectual level and being smart about what truly will shorten the equality gap between us and men. Shall we continue in our own debasement and lowering the bar to acquiesce to male dominance, we ourselves are lowering our own quality of life and for generations to come with our grandchildren and so on and thereafter. We must value ourselves beyond our looks and sex appeal. Because if we do not, men will never, and this culture of hyper-sexuality will continue and will turn into abuse, as we are already witnessing. Because when someone is viewed as an object, then it becomes easier to abuse them and discount them as a viable human being. Nothing disgusts me more than to see women who have a platform to speak out about other women being objectified and sexually abused but choose not to because they may themselves be acquiring gain through their own expression of sexuality. These women are worse than the black overseers during slavery, who made sure the other black slaves stayed in line for their masters. At least the overseer was also under the oppression of slavery itself. These powerful women are not under systemic slavery but more of their own slavery due to greed and gain.

Although men, in general, can hoe-ify us, we are in a position to not allow it by stopping our interactions with men on a level of sex and gain. Women who use their bodies are saying to themselves and the world they are nothing more than their vaginas and cannot progress in life without using their sex organs to further themselves. They are not valuing that gold card,cryptocurrency, and blockchain between their thighs. Women who are in these industries are contributing to a culture of continued female violence, continued inequality in the workplace, and continued devaluing of what women bring to our families and husbands. A husband cannot leave his home and have sex with another woman without the participation of that other woman unless it is by force… Point… Blank… Period!

The title of this book, "Be a Pussy!" And even in the opening paragraph on the topic of what women allow to be done to their vaginas can make or break them is the crux of this book and my own journey of discovery as an independent woman. Most things in life are about the woman and her vagina. Do you hear me, ladies? Are you beginning to understand the power of your pussy more now? We do not have to agree to male dominance over our pussies. We do not have to lead with our pussies and allow men to do what they will with them. IT'S OUR PUSSY!! But what we can do, is have our own pussy's best interest in mind by protecting her and using our minds to get ahead in life instead. Men have been haphazard with our pussies long enough and abused the pussy long enough. It's time for us to take our muffins back. Again, they are ours to do what we will, and using them in their most basic form is just that on the base level. Our pussies' ladies are worth far more than just sex, astronomically more. Cosmically more. When we come to this conclusion, then we will see more equality amongst men and women and true power restored back into the feminine hands of women.

Another critical suggestion is recognizing the good guys from the creeps early on. Ladies, a good man has just as high a moral standard as you do. A man who wants quality will not engage with you as a man who just wants your ass. Now, that's not to say a good guy will not accept the cookies if you are offering it to him; he is still a man. But some men will not even if you served it on a plate of gold. But this is "some" of how you can recognize a man who just wants a piece of booty, and that is all they want. This man will sexualize you very early on. I run from men who call me sexy. Yes, this is just a word, but already, that man is reducing you to your physical attributes. We have to pay attention to these things. Again, this is not to say that a man who calls you beautiful instead doesn't just want you for a good lay. There are no definitive answers here, but we must listen, pay attention and think critically, as well as give ourselves time to make up our minds about a man. Pay attention if he is pressuring you for sex. If, after just a couple weeks or a couple of months, a man is pressuring you for sex, then be alerted. And stop being such a wimp in regard to losing that man if you don't give it up so quickly. Again, no games and no 90-day formulas; I'm suggesting taking your time to decide if this man is someone you want to pursue something more with. Hell, it may take a year. It's not unheard of to go a year without sex with anyone else; talk to the throes of singles today; Handjolina has become many a man's best friend. So, do not buy into that. I can't wait, or I will die spill. Ladies, we really need to stop being cowards where our vaginas are concerned. And if he doesn't want to wait, then oh well. Again, it could take a year, or it could take a couple of months or a couple of weeks for you. To each their own, but don't be surprised with the least amount of time in those options that you figure out later that you just didn't know that man well enough and when the relationship comes to an end. Don't call that man an asshole when he high tails_it outta there after he cracks open your cherry box after a couple of weeks. He's not an ass; he just got some and left. And you gave it to him. Had you taken the time to get to know him, you might have seen that's all he wanted from you from the beginning. Let's face it: men love sex; most men want sex from us and can come on a bit strong about it. But again, pay attention to the collective of that man. If that man only calls you at night as his last priority of the day, or he never takes you anywhere but to the bedroom, or he doesn't invest and deposits into you with his time, energy, and thoughts of advice, is genuinely interested in you and shows this on a regular basis, then that man is only interested in you for sex. So, we have to be vigilant about these signals and signs. A man may want you sexually, and he may express this to you and pay attention if he is making those sacrifices for you that indicate he wants more from and with you than your body. Sacrifices that look like he's making you a top priority in his day. He is genuinely interested in getting to know you as the woman you are by asking you questions and noticing things about you that he likes. He also expresses these things to you in a healthy and mature way, that he is investing in your happiness and wants to see you happy. He may be buying you thoughtful things. He wants to make your life easier if he can by doing things for you, like going to gas up your car for you or, fixing something in your place, or at least offering. These are just some of the things that indicate a man wants more from you than just your body.

Good men have flaws and shortcomings like any other man. A good man will respect you, and if you do not feel respected and held in high esteem, and this man is frustrating you because he is behaving in a manner that upsets your equilibrium, then you need to ask yourself: why are you still with him? When a man wants you ladies for more than your ass, there is very little guessing going on. If you are feeling confused and off-kilter with this man and how he is responding to you, then he is not the man you want. And I say this because if he doesn't pursue you as you want and need, it doesn't mean he's not a good man, just not the good man you seek. You may need to move on. But be mindful also that if you are a woman used to accepting crumbs from men in past relationships, you may quite possibly be misinterpreting a good man taking it slow as he is not serious about you. Again, a good man whom you have not established a commitment with or even gotten to the level of discussing pursuing more is not going to pressure you about sex. Also, a reasonably functioning man will be open and honest with you and will be able to interact with you on a mature level. He will let you know where he stands on commitment.

One thing I follow with dating is if I find myself saying something too many times to a man I'm just starting to see and sounding like a broken record, then that man is very likely not for me. We cannot continue to try and make men become the men we need and want; he either is or is not. Recognizing this early on, before the sexual intimacy and wasting too much time, is critical. Give it time still and give the guy a fair chance, but try to remain as centered as possible and clear-minded about it. Don't get swept away with unrealistic fantasies with and about a man you do not know. So, be careful in your expectations of a man you have not established much with. Ask those questions of intentions and what he is looking for to help you determine if there is even a possibility of more down the road, as some men are not interested in anything long-term. Again, doesn't mean they are bad men unless they are lying about it to get other things from you.

I used to get so excited when I hit it off with a guy over the phone until I realized I could hit it off with just about anyone over the phone! Time and the face-to-face is the true test in ascertaining if a man is the good man that you need and want. There should be a natural progression if you are romantically inclined towards this man and you both have shared this. But not too fast. A good man will want to establish a friendship with you as you should as well with him. In this friendship stage, you need to keep it right there. Friend… ship. No, heavy petting, dry humping, kissing and all those things that will land you in someone's bedroom naked. Again, not too many expectations. If he doesn't text you every morning and night, do not get upset. This is not your man!! But surely take note of his communication style to see if it is along the lines of what you want with a partner. This is a huge mistake women make with men, is that we want that man to start acting like our Man, and we have not even established a commitment with him yet.

I know… You gals are wondering how long you go on with this man on a friendship level, and what if it never goes beyond that, but you want more? You do need to communicate with the man. Ask him periodically about his views on you as a woman. But also know this, Ladies: if you have gotten to the point that you feel you can trust this man with more and you want more, and that man is still not progressing towards pursuing you on a romantic level, then most likely a friend is all there is to this one. And this must be okay with you. This is why you do not rush into bed with a man because there just may not be anything beyond friendship, and you have great conversations with that man. This is the tricky part for us as women because we just invest too many feelings prematurely into a man who hasn't established that he wants to be in a committed relationship with us. This is also the reason why I believe in Circular Dating and having more than one male friend whom we are getting to know (on a platonic level); this is truly the definition of courting or befriending. Some men are just meant to be cool friends to us and nothing more. We just mistake our liking for each other as there is more there and because we want to be in a relationship. Some folks will make terrible partners for us, but great friends, and we have to understand this. Again, this is the reason why we take the time to get to know that man.

Another reason why I believe we need to be on this friendship/courting level with more than one man is that it helps us not to put all our emotional eggs on just that one man and too quickly. Because we can develop unrealistic expectations of that man, this helps us to live our lives and engage ourselves in other things and not become these desperate women, waiting on that one man we like to call us, text us, etc. We should not be binding ourselves emotionally to any man that we are not committed to; OMG!! I know that this line of thinking is contrary to popular belief, male-oriented belief. The male-dominated culture says as women, we need to attach ourselves to the first man who says he likes us. Well, that really has served us well. We have established that we cannot always believe what someone tells us and that it is dangerous these days to do this.

Now, if you are a woman who does want to be in a relationship with a man whom you are getting to know, that natural progression will organically unfold. A man who wants you will pursue you romantically. He may take his time, and that is fine also, but because you are a single woman and have friends, you need to remain open to the best man pursuing you. And that is what other men have to understand, is that you are not sitting around waiting on a man to make up his mind about you either. You have options. A good man understands that you are not a desperate woman. He has gotten to know you and has ascertained that you are a good woman and fit for him. He is going to swoop in on you and get you off the market as soon as possible because you both have taken that time to get to know each other. And that getting to know may come in different forms. In this day and age of social media, so much access to each other can afford us more means of getting to know each other. As I spoke of in the chapter dedicated to online media and dating, we can use our online interactions to our benefit, and if used correctly, it can allow us to meet people we would never have on our own. But some men are dense, and they do not get the desire that most women want to be properly pursued by a man whom they are interested in. Do not force the issue with those men; this becomes their loss. Tap into your other options, and if another man rises to the occasion, allow for that. Now, if you want to wait on that guy you really really like, that is on you, but also know that he may never come around to pursuing you on that level. You may be waiting a long time and may miss out on another man who suits you better anyway. So, recognizing a good man comes with getting to know that man as just a friend, and it also depends on our emotional maturity level as women and not expecting too much from a man too soon. Allowing for those concessions in being a faulty man can take a skill set in weeding out the red flags from petty differences. And with this said, know and accept that your beginnings with this man are most likely not going to be this fairytale "get along" gang experience. You are getting to know each other. We watch way too many movies and have come to believe that getting to know people should look like those movie montages of the perfection of falling into love. And although you will have some great moments with each other, we must also prepare ourselves for the not-so-great moments with each other. Moments that may end in an argument or misunderstanding. Again, know what's petty and what is not. And do not catastrophize everything. We have the tendency to see things through rose-tinted glasses early on, and when a ray of darkness splinters our contrived fantasy worlds, we think it's the end of the world or relationship, which again is why so many relationships are ending quickly these days. Yes, it can be tricky to figure out what's not a big deal and what's a deal breaker. Coming to a better understanding of this involves knowing yourself and what your wants and desires are. I have mentioned this throughout this book. And, also observing the other person you are dealing with; are they reasonable when they argue? How long does it take them to bounce back from a disagreement? Are they out of control with their anger? Do they ever apologize? Are they engaged in finding a resolution to the disagreement? Do they hold on to a grudge? Do they shut down on you? These questions and answers depend on the maturity level of both parties and what you want and desire of a partner.

I would also suggest, with the guys that wane off early on, that leave you hanging after a few texts and phone calls, who go MIA… Yes, Ladies… I told you, I know this shit! The Ghosters! Do you believe me yet? With these guys, if they come back around at some later point, I do believe it's okay to entertain them again because, although annoying, you really hadn't established too much with them. Who knows what circumstances were going on in their lives at the time of encounter with you, and who is going to tell a virtual stranger what is really going on in their lives? So, give those guys another chance, even if you deleted their numbers and blocked them online. No real harm in seeing what they have now. Proceed with caution, of course, because you are taking your time anyway, right? And if he does the same shit he did before, just be done; because you know now that's just his character. Inconsistent, which is a character trait, BTW. Move on, be a cool acquaintance. Now, I'm not referencing people you had full relationships with here; this suggestion is for those who were in the beginning phase/courting and getting to know.

My last suggestion, and probably the most important, and one I am coming to realize that sustains us as women, is our treatment of each other. Women, we have to start supporting each other more. Engaging with each other on an elevated level that truly lifts each other up. We must learn to utilize feminine energy to help take us to the next levels of our progress.

Historically, women have always depended on each other in our communities for emotional support while the men went off and pretended to do work. Well, not much has changed on that front. We still do more work with less pay and affirmation. However, we had each other to get through those tough times without our men, to get through the day-to-day of life, balancing our lives and caring for our children. But as it stands now, so many of us are barely hanging on by a thread to our sanity; panic and anxiety are ruling our lives. We are desperately trying to remain in control of the ever-growing demands of just surviving in this world we have found ourselves in, often with very little support. As single women without a significant other for support, we are at high risk of mental breakdowns, loss of control, children on the run and running the households, financial crisis, and a plethora of chaos. We must turn to other women for support. We must turn to other women for comforting words, empathy, and real help. We must organize with other women to help each other. We have to EVENTUALLY get past our ethnic differences and subcultures. These things are petty in relation to us just relating to each other as women. Now, I will interject here; there is much healing that needs to take place between various female ethnic groups FIRST, and as it stands right now, it is important for us to heal on our own first and then try to merge with other female ethnic groups. When we prematurely try to merge within a culture that is ill with dysfunction, we have the tendency to just compile our injuries, which only causes more injuries. As a black nationalist, I do believe that my own people must heal first and separate from others, and the best thing for anyone to do is to leave us alone to heal instead of trying to interject their beliefs on how we should heal with others' help. Black women need our own healing process, white women theirs, Asian women theirs, as well as Hispanic women theirs, etc. And then, at some point, possibly in HerStory we can merge our wholes to become more empowered as a feminine energy. This doesn't mean that we cannot still be allies of sorts for those who have done a significant amount of work on themselves to accept other women for where they are.

However, in general, we have to get away from the catty suspicions that have oftentimes led us in recent history. As late as the 60s, women were a united front and would come together in their households and communities. We need to find our spines and backbones again and align them with each other. We have slumbered and have been living in blissful ignorance for too long. We have to get away from the real housewives' mentality of tarring each other apart. There is very little feminine promoting about those shows, albeit entertaining, but nothing that is uplifting to women. Again, these are shown from a male perspective of how men see women. The great majority of women are disgusted with how those women behave. But again, we just go along like cattle to the slaughter and participate in our own demise. It's us women who watch those shows "in disbelief," of course. I have been guilty of it also. Then, I got rid of cable television and removed the temptation altogether to watch and promote those negative images of women. I believe to be a significant reason why we have separated from each other as women; the onset of television, online technology and social media has helped to create in us a sense of constant competition with each other to outdo the next woman.

Much of our reactions to each other have to do with what has been ingrained in us since we were little girls. We must be pretty and in competition with the other girls. Whose hair is the prettiest, who has the cutest dress on, or the most shiny shoes? All to get the boys. And television has been a big proponent of perpetuating these dangerous ideals in the name of capitalism, propaganda, and money-making agendas. We behave in these manners towards each other by route programming to attract the attention of the males. We must become privy to this knowledge and stop. It does carry over into our adult lives, and there is absolutely nothing worse than a grown azz woman who thinks she's too cute beyond reproach of how snotty her attitude is. Ladies, we do not have to behave in this manner towards each other.

Women are notorious for using that tongue of ours to cut each other to pieces, and in recent history, this has been glorified in the most inhumane of ways. We are stripping away from our femininity and what makes the spirit of the woman, who is a nurturer, peacemaker, calm-spirited, and thoughtful (generally speaking and has nothing to do with how we dress.) Again, to reference a previous chapter, not that this means we have to be docile and people pleasers either. But not the head bitch boss mentality either. That's overcompensation at best. It's easy to be dismissive and be done with people. But it takes a true woman who can lead with fairness, peace, collaboration and inclusivity with other women especially. It takes a true woman to have forgiveness and grace in her heart towards other women. It takes a woman to give another woman a compliment and mean it. To not allow other women to intimidate them by being instantly nasty towards women who intimidate them. We have to do better, ladies. Approach each other more and start a conversation. Smile at each other, and be approachable ourselves. Develop women's support groups that are positive, and be part of meet-ups with other women to connect and network with each other. Support each other in business and women-owned businesses. Get out of our comfort zones and make ourselves more vulnerable to women.

And this doesn't just apply to single women either. There are plenty of miserable women in relationships who are not being fulfilled emotionally by their men, and we can't expect men to meet all our emotional needs like this, either. That's part of some of the issues here as well. We are expecting men to complete us as we need to be completed emotionally. Yes, our men can and should meet some of our emotional needs, but they just cannot meet all of them. As women, we are the emotional beings of the two of our human species. Often, we want our men to act like us, to be just as emotional as we are, and that is just not how men were designed. But, because we are making men our universe and not surrounding ourselves with other like-minded women who can deposit into us with positive emotional support, we end up losing out. And we end up molding our men into these emotional beings who are responding just like us. And many married and booed-up women are in the same depleted state as single women.

Tapping into that camaraderie with other women is paramount if we are to grow and be more effective and balanced as women, not only for ourselves but for our children, for the men in our lives, our work and the community. What we do as women and with each other does matter, and it affects all of us. I do believe we are connected and do influence the world around us whether we want to believe it or not. What one woman does affects the world

172

and other women. Just have a discussion with Harriet Tubman, Rosa Parks, Eleanor Roosevelt, Aung San Suu Kyi, Angela Davis, and Winnie Mandela, to name a few. And many of these women were known outside and separate from the men in their lives. Even Winnie Mandela, whose husband was imprisoned for 30 years, Nelson Mandela, one of the most influential men in modern history, was still able to pave a path and walk it, herself and outside of him.

So, Miriam, what do we do with ourselves in the meantime of not having a man? We do have sexual needs; we want intimate conversations and all that. Well, Ladies, my suggestion is that you occupy your damn time! Join a gym, take up reading, join some Facebook groups, and flirt with men; you can even text and interact with men and have fun! But until it appears that man is serious about you, you better be serious about keeping your distance emotionally and physically. A relationship is a bond, a circle, a continuum. If the other person does not want to do their half and does not want to clasp hands with you to keep that circle, there is nothing you can do about it. We try to grab onto these men, hold on to them tightly, and try to make them stay. All that does is add to the struggle strain and even exhaust us after a while. So, we hold on to the people who will hold on to us. We cannot nag men into being and staying with us. But we can decide what we will accept into our lives. And let's not forget that great causes and movements started with a small number of folks in the beginning. As women, we can make a collective difference in how we are being treated in our culture today and by our men. We can learn to position ourselves without the necessary help of an immediate male in our lives. Needing a man to survive is not where any of us want to be, or a man needing you to survive is not where you want to be either. These are the things we must do as women if we want to experience growth and contentment within our lives and our purpose. I started this book as a healing process from a last failed attempt at finding the man of my dreams after I was lied to yet again by a man who told me to take a chance on him and then dropped me on my head. Well, ladies, we can only take so many drops before we learn something or just remain brain-damaged. Writing this book has helped me to tap into my creativity like so many women before me who were just disappointed in their lives and the men in their lives. I write this part with tears streaming and a heavy heart. It has been 9 years in the making of this birthing. Men are our other half in a sense, but they should never be our universe and all that we have to live for and be. In our culture, men are set up in a fashion to be the end-all and begin-all for us as women. Our ultimate goal in life is to snag us a man, and although I do believe finding a loving partner and a life partner is one of the most important decisions we can make for ourselves, our lives do not stop when we have not yet discovered that partner or when and after we have. As women, we must cultivate our own goals and aspirations outside of a man, and we cannot unfairly hold a man or our families and children to fulfill all our needs of purpose in this life. I was given a great purpose, as all of us have been given. I believe much of my purpose has to do with my writing abilities. Not all of my purpose, but some have to do with expressing myself in written word form. This is where my creativity has shown itself. I encourage all women, after reading this book and if you are like me and fell off your purpose, to tap into that thing that has given you butterflies and kept you up at night, other than that douchebag that had good game. We owe it to ourselves, our children, and our men to be happy as women, mothers and lovers. Happiness comes from within us, and we must find it by first loving the woman in that mirror. I know it's clichéish, but it's the truth. If a woman is not happy without a man, she will not be happy with a man because, again, a man cannot be held responsible to assure our happiness. That is ours, and ours alone to maintain. And when we take control of this fact, it is when we truly stop our dependency on males. Men are no longer in a position where they are to care for many and most of our needs. And many of them do not want to be placed in that position; some may want the accolades of being Superman but not the work that comes with it. But this just speaks to their shortcomings as human beings, not ours, unless we buy into it. Men are not superhuman, and we just cannot afford to stay caught up in the Lois Lane fantasy as if they are. And I believe men benefit more as well when women do not have such a desperate dependency on them. Their quality of life improves also, and they may find themselves on the golf course without too much interference from their independent women who may either be with them on the course or off doing their own damn thing! See, guys, independent women are the way to go; you will learn one day.

Most important and my last suggestion for the ladies: Get yourself a toy! A toy for that golden triangle nestled between those beautifully plump thighs of yours. Not one that's too big, though; you do not want to ruin yourself for when that "average" man does come along. Remember, he will only give you about 4-6 inches on average and remember those penis studies are primarily conducted by men, so subtract 2 inches from that. Bless their little hearts. Be very selective about what you allow to enter your shining cave of love, your womb of life, your morning muffin glory, and diamond studded pocket. It is yours and yours alone, and you are the gatekeeper.

****

*Trending Now: I have met a most interestingly, faulty, average walking wounded of a man, who is a good man… A Professor! Hmmmm. I will keep you posted…

****

Oh wait, that professor guy turned out to be a douche… Oh well, anyway! I moved to LA in 2016, And my life has opened up to so many new adventures, and the male pickings are interesting, to say the least. I met this really cool Afrocentric man the other week who… wait, that was last month… the other week, I thought this new guy was going to pan out, but he… well shit… Never Mind! I'm still single! I must add that I'm okay with it, and I'm not an alcoholic yet! Los Angeles has been treating me well. Life is good. So good I could not complete this book without adding an epilogue. See Below.

****

Epilogue:
From Pussy To (Womb) Healing…A Transformation In Progress

I started this book in August 2014, 9 years ago. It is currently August 20th, 2023, and I am completing my last independent edit of my book before I submit it for publication.

At the time of starting this book, I was disgruntled with men and what was going on with relationships between them and us women, who I thought had our shit together. And although I am still disgruntled with the single dating arena, my processing of it has changed. I was dealing with many external cues; those social cues that are very real, however, cannot affect us as deeply, if our internal cues are in order. I didn't have my shit together as much as I thought, and as this chapter notes, I am still a work in progress. I had to go into the inner walls of the pussy, THE WOMB, to find more answers. It has been a spiritual journey for me, and I am still discovering much about who I am as a woman.

As the saying goes, when the student is ready, the teacher will show up. My move to Los Angeles, California, in the summer of 2016 produced many teachers on my path, a litany of sisters and sisterhood that aligned with me in information sharing about the womb. I did not realize that, as women, we know very little about our wombs. We know about the Pussy, because that is what most men in this male-dominant culture understand it to be and where their focus is centered. And although I understood early on the power of the pussy, even our wombs, I did not have the details of the why. And more importantly, why our wombs are as sacred as they are.

This sacredness stretches back into antiquity and to the beginning of the beginning when we, as women, were deities until male dominance decided to erase our sacred history and masculinize the God source. And not to get too much into the details of my current spiritual connection. However, this is the reason why I dedicated this book to the goddess Bast, who has been my guardian angel in a sense since I was a younger woman in my 20s when I got my first and only tattoo, which is of a black panther. My career path as a social worker, working primarily with women and children, has also reflected some of this great diety's characteristics of being known as a protector of women and children. And even on to my resourceful side hustle of selling scented shea butter, to which Bast was known for her perfumed jars also. I had no idea about this great goddess until around 2018, and she has resonated with me since she came forth from my subconscious mind to my conscious mind.

Many other happenings have fallen into place for me since my move to LA, where information is just more accessible because of the diversity of people who may be willing to share it as opposed to more sheltered areas of this country. As mentioned, I have come in contact with many women who are practitioners and healers of the womb; I have attended Sister Talks and conferences on vaginal health and even intestinal health. I have found out that most of us do not even know what our vagina really looks like down there, and yes, I have even been encouraged to take a mirror and look at myself to understand this sacred place that we oftentimes allow unworthy men free access to.

On this journey that now includes a spiritual awakening about my womb and the true power source of who we are as women. We are the Sacred Feminine and have somehow allowed ourselves to fall from that place of stature. I would venture to say with the insidious nature of male dominance, this information about who we are is a feared knowing. This is one of the reasons why, as women, we have been oppressed by male dominance throughout history. Oppressed people are oppressed because of their power. Knowledge of self is what is most feared. If we come into full knowledge of self, then the power can be shifted from the oppressor to the oppressed.

In taking control of our pussies, consequently, we must include going inner and deeper into the womb. We must connect with our womb, the SACRED HER. For she is the reason for our being, for any of us. Our pussies take a beating physically at times, socially and figuratively. However, our womb is where we go to pull out the strength we need to go on. It is where we find our healing if we but understand its power, a power that transcends time and, in my beliefs, this present consciousness. That somehow, in the great scheme of the Cosmos, we women have ascended to the place of WOMBman; the gatekeepers to this Consciousness. We are the portals into this realm, where we birth whole human beings into existence. As I learn to access my own womb health more, I will share through my craft about tapping into healing from the womb. I absolutely must share this information with my girls. My writing and journaling have led me here, a place of growth. An impregnation that has filled me, and as I have stated early on in this book, over 9 years of scribing, we cannot experience growth without changing our minds and producing something. I hope you were literally able to feel my growth in my penning this book. This was a birthing for me with various stages. I have grown in understanding the pussy is powerful, yet the WOMB is sacred and magical; it is where authentic feminine healing must begin. Be a Pussy and embrace the core of your womb that makes you a GODdess.

M.

NOT THE END!

Made in the USA
Columbia, SC
28 April 2024

d543008f-4b3f-4892-8754-1a640bc9e312R02